*"Little Keys Open Big Doors* addressing change at every level and what it takes to achieve change. All who read this book will be challenged to press forward with a whole heart. The section on dreams—from owning your dreams to birthing them and all the phases in between—is a must-read. This book will be a comprehensive life guide for those who hunger and thirst for the reality of the Kingdom of God in their lives."

—**Chuck D. Pierce**, president, Glory of Zion International; watchman, Global Harvest Ministries

"Just as Jacob's son Joseph had the ability to speak the language of both the Hebrews and the Egyptians, Rachel's deep experiences in both the Eastern and the Western worlds gives her a unique perspective to address an issue sorely lacking in the Church today. Her revelatory insight concerning intercession and her depth of experience in the walk of faith give her a unique ability to challenge us to move to the next level of supernatural breakthrough. Every intercessor, leader and pastor will grow as we follow Rachel through a refreshing journey of practical insights that prepare us for seeing what the Father has in His heart for His Church."

—**Bishop Joseph Garlington**, senior pastor, Covenant Church, Pittsburgh

"Rachel Hickson is a woman of prayer and wisdom. Burdened for the spiritual state of our nations, she stirs us in her new book to a fresh hunger for God. Challenging, inspiring and full of practical insights."

—**Colin Dye**, senior minister, Kensington Temple, London; leader, London City Church Network

"With the clear call of a clarion trumpet, Rachel Hickson has penned a provocative prophetic summons to the people of God. The call is the cry to experience breakthrough into supernatural realms for the sake of the generations to come. Rachel's intercessory passion, coupled with deep biblical insights, encourages believers in a practical and systematic way to awaken from spiritual slumber and to dream again. If you've been sensing the restless longing for something deeper in your walk with the Lord, this book will kindle the inner fires of your heart for deep and lasting change leading to supernatural breakthrough!"

—**Dr. Wendell Smith**, pastor, The City Church of Seattle

"This is a dangerous book. It is a threat to our complacency and a weapon against Satan's stealing our destiny. As I read it, I could sense a new fresh fire burning in my heart to see the nations transformed. Rachel's vulnerability made me laugh and feel convicted all at once! God will use it to raise up a new generation of lovers of God and world changers."

—**Cindy Jacobs**, Generals International

"Rachel Hickson is one of those unique people who can soar into the highest realms of spiritual life through prayer and intercession, and then, through biblical balance and practical living, walk out the insights gained. This book will inspire your vision to soar and equip your feet to walk it out. Rachel, great job once again! You are a friend, a great leader and a precious gift to the Body of Christ."

—**Frank Damazio**, senior pastor, City Bible Church, Portland

"Rachel Hickson is the real deal—inspirationally passionate, eloquent and courageous, yet reassuringly warm, practical and 'earthed' as well. I'm glad to commend her ministry."

—**Pete Greig**, founder, 24-7 Prayer

# Little Keys
# Open Big Doors

*Secrets to Experiencing Breakthrough
in Every Area of Life*

Rachel Hickson

**Chosen**
Grand Rapids, Michigan

Published by Chosen Books
A division of Baker Publishing Group
P.O. Box 6287, Grand Rapids, MI 49516-6287
www.chosenbooks.com

Originally published under the title *Supernatural Breakthrough: The Heartcry for Change* by New Wine Ministries of West Sussex, England

Printed in the United States of America

        Library of Congress Cataloging-in-Publication Data
Hickson, Rachel.
    Little keys open big doors : secrets to experiencing breakthrough in
    every area of life / Rachel Hickson.
        p. cm.
    ISBN 10: 0-8007-9415-X (pbk.)
    ISBN 978-0-8007-9415-6 (pbk.)
    1. Christian life.    I. Title.
    BV4501.3.H525 2007
    243—dc22
                                                2007021720

Unless otherwise indicated, Scripture is taken from the HOLY BIBLE, NEW INTERNATIONAL VERSION®. NIV®. Copyright © 1973, 1978, 1984 by International Bible Society. Used by permission of Zondervan. All rights reserved.

Scripture marked NKJV is taken from the New King James Version. Copyright © 1982 by Thomas Nelson, Inc. Used by permission. All rights reserved.

Scripture marked KJV is taken from the King James Version of the Bible

I dedicate this book to three groups of pioneers for change:

The History Makers of Yesterday
*The Pioneers of Change*

To men like George Whitefield, John and Charles Wesley, William Wilberforce and Evan Roberts; and to women like Gladys Aylward, Elizabeth Fry and Florence Nightingale, who by their courage and determination showed us that change is possible and little people can make a difference.

The Nation Shakers of Today
*The Messengers of Action*

To men like Reinhard Bonnke, who have preached the message and seen Africa saved; to women like Jackie Pullinger, who have challenged the drug culture of Hong Kong and seen the drug lords repent and the Walled City fall; to heroes like Rolland and Heidi Baker, who have served the war-torn nation of Mozambique and loved her children; and to the many other leaders of today.

The Destiny Holders of Tomorrow
*The Dreamers of Big Dreams*

To the next generation of history writers, our children and grandchildren who will not sit down but who want to change their world; to people like Tim Douglass, my son-in-law, who has left Australia and come to Europe to see the youth of capital cities touched with the presence of God; to my "Baton Catchers," a group of young people determined to touch the world of arts, theater, films and the media and connect it back to the Church.

And to everyone with a dream for tomorrow,

Dream big and write the next pages of history for us!

# Contents

# Acknowledgments

This is always the hardest part of a book to write! How can you really say an adequate "thank you" to all the amazing people who help you write and encourage you to birth your dreams? But there are special people who do deserve a BIG thank you! Once again I need to thank Tim Pettingale for all his knowledge and advice and for pushing me to write. So, now the second book is written due to his persistent patience and encouragement.

I also need to thank my family: Gordon, David, Nicola and Tim, who have allowed me to write and even tell some of their story in this book. I need to thank Helen Azer and Gordon for reading the manuscript in detail and giving me advice, corrections and lots of encouragement— thank you! This has all given me confidence to go to print once again.

But I need to thank so many incredible people all over the world who have challenged me to never let go of my dreams and learn how to break through. I need to thank Reinhard Bonnke for showing me keys of breakthrough in nations and for praying for me to live in 1984. I need to thank my parents, Alan and Eileen Vincent, for living a life of breakthrough and faith concerning finances. I need to thank the churches of London for persisting and praying for our great city to be changed.

Finally, I need to thank you for buying this book. I trust that the words of this book will help you become a person who lives dangerously, births your dreams and breaks through into a new place of freedom.

Rachel Hickson
April 2007

# SECTION 1

## *The Heartcry for Change*

# The Cry for Change

*"A season to comfort the afflicted and afflict the comfortable."*
—Unknown

## Introduction

Today as we look at the state of our world, from nations in political and spiritual turmoil to the unrest in many homes in our neighborhoods, a deep cry should stir within our hearts: "O God, please help us. We need to change!" I feel this heartcry most acutely when I see the pain and confusion on the faces of little children. Surrounded by foul language, selfishness and anger, most look fearful rather than loved, and my heart cries out for the next generation: "God, we need change; we need a visitation of Jesus in our streets."

I long to see the kind of change that will see hard hearts turned to God; governments and industry campaigning for righteous standards once again; politicians who love the people of their communities more than their power; wealthy business-people who love God more than their money. We need change—deep, radical change, change that works from the inside out—the type of change that is written first upon the hearts of men, women and children and then worked into the statute books and enshrined in law.

If we are to see the next generation living with a sense of hope and the promise of a future, then we, the Church of today, need to cry out: "O God, have mercy." We need to work together to see a supernatural breakout and breakthrough of the blessing of God. I want to be a part of a generation that starts a movement for change, beginning on our knees with the cry, "O God, change us and let us be messengers of this change," and ending on our feet carrying this message into the community as ambassadors of change.

I believe that together we can see the kind of radical change that so many long for. In this book I invite you to walk the journey of change with me and discover God's keys for supernatural breakthrough in the resistant areas until we see the breakout of His presence in our streets. Let us begin to move with a heartcry for change! As you continue reading, allow God to challenge you and let Him trigger in you a raw desperation for something new, a desperation that will cause you to pay the price for change.

## The Hannah hour

Not too long ago, God woke me up early one morning with the following message: *Rachel, this is the season of Hannah for the Church.* I was familiar with the story of Hannah as told in chapter one of 1 Samuel, but I was curious to understand what was on God's heart, so I began to study this story in more depth. As I studied this passage of Scripture again and again and allowed God to speak to me, I became convinced that it carries a message of vital importance for the Western Church today. I believe the Church needs to embrace this season of the

"Hannah hour." The essence of this Hannah message can be summarized by the following statement:

*A cry of desperation needs to lead us to a new level of sacrifice, and this sacrifice will birth a season of change and breakthrough.*

I want to highlight certain key attitudes in the life of Hannah that caused her intense desperation. Hannah illustrates what our response must be on this journey of change.

We read in 1 Samuel 1 that Hannah had a husband whose name was Elkanah, who came from the tribe of Ephraim. Biblical names and places of origin often give us insight and understanding about a person's spiritual heritage, and this is certainly true in Hannah's story. People's names, family heritage and the places where they are born and then live all carry significance to God, because He does nothing by accident. God preordains our geography and our family ties for a purpose. Genesis 41:52 tells us that Joseph had a son whom he named "Ephraim" and explains the reason for giving him that name: "The second son he named Ephraim and said, 'It is because God has made me fruitful in the land of my suffering.'"

Elkanah, then, came from a household with a family inheritance of fruitfulness. In fact, the literal meaning of *Ephraim* is "double fruitfulness born in a time of suffering." How ironic then that here he is married to a woman he loves deeply but who so far has been unable to bear him a child. It was as if Elkanah's family name and heritage now mocked him. How many of us also live with this longing for fruitfulness in our lives? Yet we encounter fierce opposition as we dare to step into our destiny. We have the promise of God, but still our lives carry the pain and conflict of a lack of fruitfulness. If that is your experience, then you need to know that whatever God has declared over you *will* become your final experience—you will see and touch the promise of God in time. Each one of us must engage in this season of Hannah, knowing that we will see our circumstances ultimately break through to *fruitfulness*, but there will be sacrifices to endure before the fruitfulness comes. God eventually made Hannah fruitful, but it came out of a place of trial.

First Samuel 1:3 tells us that year after year Elkanah traveled with his two wives, Hannah and Peninnah, from their home-town to worship the Lord and offer sacrifices at Shiloh. It was their annual pilgrimage to meet with God, perhaps a bit like Christian conferences in our yearly calendars. They went as a family and sought God together, but the subsequent verses give us a penetrating insight into the relationships between these three people:

> Whenever the day came for Elkanah to sacrifice, he would give portions of the meat to his wife Peninnah and to all her sons and daughters. But to Hannah he gave a double portion because he loved her, and the LORD had closed her womb. And because the LORD had closed her womb, her rival kept provoking her in order to irritate her. This went on year after year.
>
> 1 Samuel 1:4–7

As the story unfolds we discover that Hannah is *desperate* to bear a child, but at present she is "unfruitful." Not only that, but her rival in love has borne a number of children for Elkanah already. As if this were not enough, Peninnah chooses to ridicule and mock Hannah about her barrenness. Verse 7 makes the telling statement that this went on "year after year." Do you have circumstances in your life that have been relentlessly unchanging, year after year? Are there situations that are continually provoking you, irritating you? Every year Hannah went up to have time to meet with God, but there was always this shadow of pain. Though Hannah was loved, she was not fruitful, and Peninnah was quick to point out this fact.

I believe at this time God is allowing certain "Peninnahs" to work in our lives to provoke us out of our comfort zones—especially those of us who belong to the Western Church. God is using situations to shake us from our complacency and spur us into action. We have become so accustomed to our barrenness and our lack of fruitfulness that we are immune to the facts, and we accept these circumstances as "normal." Perhaps in the past God promised us that others in our family would be saved, but each year nothing seems to change and we just grow accustomed to the hardness of our relatives' hearts and lose the expectation of change. Maybe we hear of people we know who are ill, and we feel we should pray for their healing, but they get worse and perhaps even die. Because we have conditioned ourselves to put up with a state of barrenness, we just walk on, accepting the status quo. Rather than accept her circumstances, something happened to Hannah. One year her response to her situation was very different: A cry for change stirred within her.

Notice in these verses that it was the Lord who had the final word on Hannah's condition: "And because the LORD had closed her womb, her rival kept provoking her in order to irritate her. This went on year after year" (verses 6–7).

God was the one who had closed her womb. Later when He decided to open her womb, no devil could keep her barren. The Lord was well aware of Peninnah and the relationship between her, Hannah and their husband. But Peninnah's constant provoking was a necessary instrument in that land of suffering from which fruitfulness would be birthed.

I believe that at this time in our nation God is doing something to put Peninnahs in our path. Both as individuals and corporately as the Church, we need to understand why God is allowing this, what He is saying to us through these situations and how we are to respond.

Hannah must have become so tired of Peninnah's constant needling. The very sound of her voice must have instantly irritated Hannah. I do not know what your Peninnah sounds like, but there are certain sounds and situations that have begun to irritate me seriously. As I read some of the recent legislation being passed by governments concerning family life, marriage and our children's education, these decisions provoke me to cry out. I feel provoked by my lack of authority to bring change where it really matters. Another area that has bothered me for a long time is the lack of signs, wonders, miracles and demonstrations of the awesome power of God poured out in our churches and our nations. We the Church have become barren and have lost our "children" of signs and wonders! I think that many believers in the Western Church are like Hannah, who made her annual trips to Shiloh. Year after year we find ourselves in "conference season." We go to the house of the Lord looking for something new to satisfy us. We visit our Shilohs and are blessed, perhaps with a double portion. But there are others who are quick to highlight and expose our lack of fruitfulness and provoke us about our lack of power. They challenge us to do something about it, but very quickly the sting of the challenge is over and we go back home. Nothing has really changed. Year after year the same pattern continues. Yes, we may be blessed, but I believe we are coming into the days when intimacy is no longer enough. God is provoking us to fruitfulness!

Hannah began to be desperate for fruitfulness. She reached a place where she would weep and refuse to eat whenever she was provoked. Elkanah tried to soothe and console her, but to no avail. In verse 8 he said, effectively, "Hannah, why are you weeping? Why don't you eat? Why are you downhearted? Look! You are blessed. Doesn't this mean more than ten sons?" Well, Hannah's answer was simple: She was silent. Within her began to rage a deep dissatisfaction, a cry for change. Inside she said to herself, *No, blessing is NOT enough. I have to have fruitfulness.* Even though her husband loved her so much and blessed her with a double portion of blessing, this was not enough to satisfy her; she needed more—she needed children of promise born from the place of intimacy!

If you have seen any of the *Transformations* videos and responded like me, then they will have provoked you. But I really hope that we do not keep watching these videos of revival breaking through in the nations year after year, being provoked by them, and never experiencing for ourselves the amazing works of God in our own nation. There is something in me that cries, "God, I am not satisfied with what I see! I'm provoked!" Even the *Transformations* videos—and I mean this most respectfully—have become a Peninnah to me! I hope they will begin to irritate and provoke you, too, to disturb your comfort zone to the extent that you will no longer be able to sit down and simply enjoy the double portion blessing of Shiloh year after year.

Our Western nations desperately need an outpouring of God's power. I have become desperate to see such an outpouring. Like Hannah I long for the cry of our hearts to be, "Lord, give us our children or we will die!" What "child" do you want to bring to birth? In other words, what is the destiny, the promise that God has called you to birth in this land in this season?

If we are honest, most of us are lazy! We know that the spiritual state of our nation is not what it should be, and we know that we could do something about it. We know we ought to be praying about it more. Most of us want to pray, we know we must pray and we believe we should be desperate, but we are just not. So, before we will ever break through in our nation, we need to reach a new level of brokenness and desperation about its state. This is the place that Hannah had reached by verse 7 of 1 Samuel 1. Something exploded within her spiritually and emotionally that caused her to shout out, "No! I can't tolerate this anymore!" Maybe a more natural reaction to Peninnah's tormenting ways would be to want to kill her. But Hannah did not choose to vent her anger directly against her adversary; rather, she allowed this provocation to fuel her determination to get her into the right place before God.

Some of you reading this book right now will undoubtedly have Peninnahs in your life that you would like to get rid of. In your mind you have issued a writ of execution upon your Peninnah and plan to put it to death as soon as possible! But I believe God will keep that Peninnah alive because His intent is for those circumstances to bring you into a right place in Him— a place where your desperation for Him to act will eventually blossom into fruitfulness. The truth is, God often works profoundly in us during seasons of suffering. Those seasons allow Him to touch deep areas of our lives where we would never choose to go except in crisis time. When God brings you to a place of holy desperation, all other priorities melt into insignificance. Hannah did not sit down with her schedule and think, *I really need to plan a time of serious prayer and fasting about this matter.* It was not a planned, neatly scheduled prayer time, and it went beyond natural reasoning. She was so distressed that she lost her appetite. Eating was no longer a priority. Nothing else mattered anymore. She was focused, and she needed to see a breakthrough and a change.

By contrast, recognizing that there are troubles in our nation and knowing that we need to pray, we may well sit down with our schedules and see if we can find a convenient slot for some extra prayer. *Maybe I can grab a bit of time here?* we think. *That would be suitable and not too inconvenient! Oh no, hang on, I've got a wedding to go to then.* And so on. In the end all the demands in our lives crowd in and stifle our good intentions, so we never find a convenient time when we can commit to a time of fasting and prayer.

Hannah did not think this way. She was devastated. Perhaps before we ever come to a place of desperation we need to experience devastation. Are we devastated enough by the state of our nation? By the crime, promiscuity, teenage pregnancies, abortion? I do not think I am, and I gently suggest that maybe you're not either. Once we get devastated about something, that becomes our all-consuming priority. Hannah's barrenness became her priority because she realized her real loss, and thus came the cry of devastation. She had to accept the reality: "I am barren. . . . Peninnah has children. . . . I *don't* have children, and it *does matter* to me."

Sometimes we comfort ourselves by saying, "Maybe it doesn't really matter if we don't see God's supernatural power poured out here as in other nations. God's doing good things; we have some unity in our cities; some things are coming together." It is true, everything is not negative and good things are happening here and there, but aren't we just sticking our heads in the sand by telling ourselves things are not that bad? Of course we are! That is why God will be forced to use some Peninnahs to get our attention and cause us to wake up!

I find myself being stirred by God at this time: "Come on, Rachel, come on! Get rid of all the games. Let's look at what really matters." Do you know what I have discovered? This is what really matters to me: the souls of men, women and children, and seeing signs, wonders and miracles in my nation. I want to see this with every fiber of my being.

The fact is, I am alive today only because of the powerful

prayers of radical, totally committed believers who held on to
God for my miracle and refused to allow me to die. In 1984 I
was in Zimbabwe working as a missionary when I was run over
by a seven-ton military truck. I was picked up off the road and
taken to a hospital where I was almost certain to die, the
doctors said, because my injuries had caused multiple fat
emboli. Yet there was a church in Zimbabwe that was prepared
to pray for me. They did not pray prayers like, "Dear God, if it's
Your will, let Rachel live." They got desperate. They were
devastated by my accident. I had been in Africa for only six
weeks and so had no real, deep relationships with any of the
people there yet, but still I mattered to them. The very fact that
I would leave my home to go to minister alongside them,
that my husband would sell his business, that we would arrive
in Africa with a four-month-old baby and were prepared to sow
our lives into their land—that was enough for them to get
desperate before God. Around-the-clock prayer meetings were
established in five churches across the city where we lived. I
was told later that there was never less than one thousand
people, day and night, crying out to the Father, "God, give
us Rachel!"

Five days later my father walked into the hospital to be by
my bedside, where I lay in a coma. An earlier phone call from
the hospital had warned him to come prepared to collect my
body. On top of the many prayers of God's faithful ones across
the city and at home in England, my dad simply prayed over
me, "Rachel, you shall not die but live. And you will declare the
words the Lord has spoken." Five hours later I awoke from
the coma, totally conscious and in my right mind. God had
completely and dramatically healed me.

It is time to change our priorities. Intimacy can satisfy us for
only so long, but then life must be born from us. *All intimacy is
designed to lead to fruitfulness.* Year after year, Hannah denied the

cry for life that she knew was deep within her. We must not do the same! We must let the cry for life be released. It really matters to me that we do not regularly see signs, wonders and miracles in all our churches accompanying the preaching of the Word. It does irritate me that we have to go to Uganda, Kenya, Nigeria and South America to see these signs, while our Western nations have become barren.

First Samuel 1:9–10 are significant verses which highlight the change in Hannah's heart: "Once when they had finished eating and drinking in Shiloh, Hannah stood up.... In bitterness of soul Hannah wept much and prayed to the LORD."

First of all, Hannah stood up (verse 9). She instigated a change of posture, of position. The Church has been sitting down for too long! It is time to stand up and take our responsibility. Hannah suddenly stood up in the midst of all the Shiloh celebrations and took responsibility for what she knew was inside her. We, too, must take responsibility for what God has put inside us—that which we know God has called us to do.

Secondly, the irritation of Hannah's rival had finally provoked her to *desperation*. In recent years the Church has been touched by an outpouring of the Spirit known by many as "the Toronto Blessing." We have experienced a season of great intimacy with the Father, when many have been brought into a new place of healing and wholeness in their identity. But I believe that this season was a comma rather than a period, or a full stop. This season was part of a journey, not an end in itself. God does not want us to remain there, yet we have found a comfort zone in this place of blessing. Now it is time to leave the comfort zone, be stirred and move into a season of desperation. God has healed and touched our broken hearts. Now it is time for us to work with Him for the broken lives of thousands of others.

Like Hannah, we have to begin to bow down and pour out our souls. God wants us to enter a season of tears—not tears of self-pity but tears of a heart that is engaging once again with the Father's heart for our people, our land, our barrenness. I believe that God wants us to express the deep desires He has put within us. In her time of weeping Hannah began to pray and made a vow before the Lord:

> "O LORD Almighty, if you will only look upon your servant's misery and remember me, and not forget your servant but give her a son, then I will give him to the LORD for all the days of his life, and no razor will ever be used on his head."
>
> 1 Samuel 1:11

Hannah kept on praying and refused to give up. The people around her misunderstood her. They thought she was fanatical, totally over the top. She was so distressed in her soul that Eli, her leader, could not recognize this was God and so assumed she was drunk! I believe now is a time for such "excess" in the Church. I am not saying we should all become alcoholics! What I mean is, God is stirring something in us to shake us out of our complacency. We English are perhaps the worst at this: stiff upper lip, let's keep everything looking nice, orderly and under control, please! Well, I believe there is going to be some coloring outside the lines, some untidiness in Jesus' name, some mascara running down our pretty faces and some red noses and puffy eyes. Not a pretty sight to us, but very precious in the sight of God. The Church needs to stir!

Hannah responded to Eli and said, "No, Eli you've got it wrong. . . ."

> "I am a woman who is deeply troubled. I have not been drinking wine or beer; I was pouring out my soul to the LORD.

Do not take your servant for a wicked woman; I have been
praying here out of my great anguish and grief."

1 Samuel 1:15–16

In my own prayer life I feel I am at the place where I need to
pray, "God, give me the grace to feel the grief and anguish that I
need to feel in order to change." At the moment I cannot even
pour my heart out to God properly because I do not feel
connected enough to His heart. This is desperation! But out of
the place of desperation comes *conception*. Naturally speaking,
you would not expect this to be a time when Hannah would
conceive. But through this time of anguish she did conceive!
Hannah conceived after desperation:

> Early the next morning they arose and worshiped before the
> LORD and then went back to their home at Ramah. Elkanah lay
> with Hannah his wife, and the LORD remembered her. So in the
> course of time Hannah conceived and gave birth to a son.
> She named him Samuel, saying, "Because I asked the LORD
> for him."
>
> 1 Samuel 1:19–20

I want to challenge you: when was the last time that you lay
desperate in the presence of God? When you look at your
neighbors, your community, your city—what is your response?
I believe that God is calling us to a season of prayer that is
much deeper and more mature than quick fix-it prayers. This
is an "asking" prayer born out of anguish and grief for the state
of the lost, a desperation that demands something be super-
naturally conceived—a child of promise that will break the
barrenness of the spiritual atmosphere across your city.

After conception and birth comes *sacrifice*. Verses 27–28 of
1 Samuel 1 reveal another twist in Hannah's amazing story:

"I prayed for this child, and the LORD has granted me what I asked of him. So now I give him to the LORD. For his whole life he will be given over to the LORD."

Are you prepared to give away what you are being called to birth with sacrifice? In the coming days I believe God will challenge us to give up some of the things that we have seen birthed—those "babies" born in our season of sacrificial pain for the sake of the community. For one, I believe God is going to seriously challenge us about our attitudes toward money. Many churches I know are praying about the release of finance for building projects. Well, maybe God will challenge you to give away the money that seems to be yours for the sake of His Kingdom. Most people would acknowledge that money is one of the strongholds of our Western nations. In order to bring a stronghold down, we need to come against it with an opposite spirit. Where there is greed and selfishness, we must come with openness and generosity.

If you are a pastor, you can imagine the possible reactions of your eldership team when your church, which has been praying and fasting for weeks for a financial breakthrough, suddenly receives a large amount of money for the building project and you decide you must give it away to the church down the road. They may well think you have gone crazy, yet this is real Kingdom thinking. The bottom line is that it is not just about your name, your reputation and your project, but the breakthrough of the whole. These are the kind of things with which God is going to confront us. If we choose to ignore these challenges, then we will simply start the process again until devastation and desperation lead us back to the opportunity of sacrifice once again, and we obey.

Hannah could have kept Samuel for herself, and it would have broken the barrenness in her household and her life. But what did she choose to do? She sacrificed Samuel and gave her gift of breakthrough to benefit her country. She saw the bigger picture and broke the barrenness of a nation. The Word of the Lord had been absent from the land, and then came Samuel—a prophet who carried the Word of God for the land. Before Samuel began his ministry, the Word of the Lord was rare in the land; once he began to speak, the whole nation heard the voice of a prophet once again.

In my own life God has asked me to make many sacrifices, especially regarding my family time. In order to have the privilege of touching nations, my family has had to sacrifice precious time that we could have enjoyed with each other. It costs, but our reward has been in the nations. Just as Hannah gave up Samuel, I have had to release my family.

I have a wonderful mom and dad. I love them dearly. But as a little girl growing up in India, I was sent off to boarding school at age nine and saw my parents for only three weeks each May, nine weeks each December/January, and ten days each August. This was my home life from age nine to sixteen. Somehow I never resented it because I knew that God was using my parents, but there were many times when I cried in loneliness and wanted a "normal" home. That said, I understood deep inside, even as a child, that God was asking us to make sacrifices as a family.

Nevertheless, I grew up with a romantic dream that one day we would all live close to one another, see each other regularly and be together as a family. In due course I got married and we lived in England, just down the road from my parents, for almost two years. But then God called Gordon and me to serve Him in Africa alongside Reinhard Bonnke. We sold our company and everything we had, and we lived in Africa for the next six and a half years. Nicola was young when we left, and David, my second child, was born on the mission field. I had dreamed that we would all live close together when I had my children, but again the call of God had moved me so that we lived thousands of miles apart. But we knew we had to go, so we went, and at times we did cry!

Then it was my children who had a dream! They dreamed of returning to England and living next door to Granny and Granddad again and living happily ever after. After almost seven years in Africa, we returned to England in October of 1990, and it looked as though we would all be together again, but the reality of this dream was short-lived. Just a couple of months later, in December, my parents informed us that God had called them to sell the family home and move to San Antonio, Texas. "We're selling and moving to America," Dad said. At that moment everything in me screamed, "No! It's not fair!" But I knew I would have no option but to release them. So in due course they moved to San Antonio.

A few years later on New Year's Day of 2000 my father phoned me. We were just chatting, and he said, "Happy New Year, Rachel." Then he simply stated, "We've bought our burial plots. We will live and serve God here."

"Happy New Year to you, too, Dad!" I said quickly, a little shocked by the finality of this statement.

He continued. "We're taking American citizenship."

At that moment it hit me. That little girl's dream I had held on to for so long was never going to come true. I was going to have to lay it on the altar of God. I had wanted my parents to come home and help us with the churches we pastored in Britain and to be a spiritual voice in the United Kingdom. But God challenged me: *Rachel, they are not yours—give them away.* God challenged me to let go of all my spiritual expectations and sentimental longings. To be honest with you, I really struggled with the loss of my parents to America. Did I really want my mom and dad to become American citizens? My immediate response was no! My mom and dad are both in their seventies, and I knew this type of radical decision meant they were never coming back to live in the United Kingdom. They would never partner with us in the United Kingdom in the way I had imagined for revival and spiritual breakthrough. I was going to have to grow up, take my responsibility, find my own destiny and fulfill my task in my nation.

But God has His ways of helping us come to terms with things. I was invited out to San Antonio to speak at a citywide prayer event called "Three Days of Glory." My mom and dad were there, and people from a number of different churches had gathered for this event. I was asked to speak on Saturday evening, and while I was preaching God said to me, *Rachel, I want you to let go of your mom and dad now. Give them to San Antonio for the sake of My Kingdom, because you have not really let them go.* So I did, publicly in that meeting. Immediately people began to cry, and a new strength of relationship was formed between my family and these people in San Antonio. As a direct result, I believe, the presence of God in that meeting was extraordinary. It had nothing to do with me! But it had everything to do with a sacrifice of obedience.

That is a small part of my journey. In order to see God break out in power I have had to make sacrifices. My sacrifices have been many and varied—sometimes the holiday I wanted to have, the car I wanted to drive, the place I wanted to live, the house I wanted to own, the family I wanted to love. All these things are not wrong in their own right, but I have had to let go and let God have His way. Your sacrifice will be different, but we all need to learn to come to the place of the altar of sacrifice if we are going to see God's power break out. We may have to sacrifice our dreams, our longings, our hopes, our traditions, our reputations, our likes and dislikes, our culture— because it is time for the Hannah hour of desperation and sacrifice.

## Hannah's prayer

At the beginning of the second chapter of 1 Samuel we read Hannah's prayer to the Lord. It begins, "My heart rejoices in the LORD," and continues with great exuberance. Considering all that she has gone through and the fact that she ultimately had to give up the child she so longed for, Hannah's prayer is truly astonishing.

She is filled with sheer joy. Joy? Yes, because she sees beyond all that she has suffered to the joy of fruitfulness, the day of breakthrough. The Bible says that those who sow in tears shall reap with joy. Hannah is overwhelmed with joy, even though she has given away the most precious gift imaginable to her.

In the next chapter of 1 Samuel we see the young boy Samuel ministering before the Lord under Eli the priest and God calling him into His service. The beginning of this chapter underlines the barren state of the nation at the time. We read, "The word of the LORD was rare in those days; there was no widespread revelation" (1 Samuel 3:1, NKJV).

The nation was spiritually barren, and Eli, the one who should have been speaking the Word of the Lord to the people, was blind. His physical sight was failing, but his greater problem was his spiritual blindness. The Hebrew sense of the word for a prophet is "seer," but here the prophet of Israel was blind and unable to "see" and so fulfill his God-given task. We also know that Eli's sons were not following God, and they had become careless with the presence of God. So the nation was barren, their designated spiritual leader was blind and unable to lead effectively and there was no hope when looking at the next generation of prophets. Into this atmosphere the boy Samuel emerges. But in this passage one phrase stands out to me, and I want to emphasize this phrase: *"The lamp of God had not yet gone out"* (1 Samuel 3:3).

I believe that God is still being merciful to us in the Western Church, and although our society has become godless and the Church has lost its spiritual vision in many places, God has still not given up on His Church. The prophetic voice may seem silent, the scent of the fresh bread of the Word of God in the land may be rare, but God is still watching over our nations. Although I know we are in severe trouble, I also thank God that His lamp has not yet gone out over the Western Church. While the light of God still shines, there is always hope for the land.

In recent times we have seen numerous disasters strike various parts of the world, and dreadful things have happened in our nation. People ask me, "Rachel, are we in judgment? What is happening?" I do not believe that we are living in the days of the final judgment yet, but I do believe that we are under the rebuke of the Lord. Hebrews 12:6 says, "The Lord disciplines those he loves." Our nations are based upon covenants with God, and I believe God is saying, "You have forgotten your covenant with Me, and so I must bring discipline upon you."

What covenant does my nation have with God, you might ask? Well, if you look closely at the constitutions of our governmental systems in the West, you will see that the whole basis for our societies is established upon various covenants with God in line with biblical values. These principles run through the judicial system, the constitution, the police force, the health service, the prison service and nearly every area of public life. These institutions were founded by or with the Church as the main influence. Yet we have forgotten that God is part of our heritage and culture, and we have now broken the moral and ethical codes of the Bible.

So it is time for the Church to wake up! It is time for the Church to get desperate! Is there moral barrenness in our nation? Yes, there is, so we need to become desperate and cling to God in the place of both prayer and action until we see the situation reversed. Our prayers and our words must go beyond our own private world and become unselfish. Hannah gave birth to Samuel, but she did not try to keep him for herself; she gave him away for the benefit of a nation.

In 1 Samuel 3:19–21 we read that the Lord was with Samuel and blessed him greatly:

> The LORD was with Samuel as he grew up, and he let none of his words fall to the ground. And all Israel from Dan to Beersheba recognized that Samuel was attested as a prophet of the LORD. The LORD continued to appear at Shiloh, and there he revealed himself to Samuel through his word.

The opening verse of the following chapter says very simply, "And Samuel's word came to all Israel" (4:1).

Condensed into this one chapter of the Bible we see a rapid transformation, where the barrenness of the land is broken and God's voice begins to sound in the nation again. At the beginning of 1 Samuel 3 there is no Word of the Lord, no revelation. But by the beginning of chapter 4 the Word of the Lord is touching the entire nation. Because the sacrifice was made, the transformation could take place.

The challenge for us, then, is this: What are our Peninnahs? What are those things that provoke and irritate us and make us realize that the status quo is no longer acceptable? What are we going to do about our personal and corporate barrenness? Are we going to continue to live with it as Hannah did for many years? Or are we going to let God provoke in us a movement for change? What are the areas in which we are resistant to change? Unfortunately, so often in the Church we find that the last move of God is the first to resist the next move of God. We forget so quickly, and we who were the pioneers of change in our generation become the voices that criticize the next movement of change that needs to touch the Church. Ask God to show you if you have become stuck in old ways and have grown familiar with wrong attitudes.

I believe we are living in a season in which God is allowing the ridicule and the provocation of our rivals to increase, because in His graciousness he is provoking His Church into the right place. This is a place of prayer connected to action, a place of desperation that will lead to the conception of a new vision and a place of sacrifice that will ultimately see the barrenness of our land being broken.

Our comfort zones need to be devastated. There is a different level of prayer that God is calling us to enter into, and we need to learn this language—this prayer that changes situations—because we the Church become the answer to our own prayers! So I am praying and asking God, "Lord, teach me the cry of the Hannah hour. Teach me how to get desperate." I am on a learning curve in this area of my life, and I need a new encounter with God so that I have a shift in my thinking. I pray that you, too, will connect with God in this way and begin to pray like Hannah did. I believe we need to see a radical change, but are we willing to pay the price? Does the state of the nation matter to us? Or have we become so immune to the pain of people's lives and the godlessness in our society that we have blinded our eyes and keep on living as if everything is fine? We cannot afford to do that. This is a time for change!

# The Cost of Change

*"Organizations only change when the people in them change,
and people will only change when they accept
in their hearts that change must occur."*
—Sir John Harvey-Jones, former chairman of ICI Corporation

## All change! All change!

Once the desire for change has been stirred and a deep desperation for something new has been activated, we need to evaluate our life, identifying where change needs to occur. Often as we turn our attention to the practical implications of changes we need to make, we begin to realize the cost of the process and become afraid to pay the price. We can easily withdraw and hide behind our "safe" routines, fearful of upsetting the pleasant status quo. But we must recognize that although there is a cost to change, we will lose so much more if we shrink back from it. Rather than thinking about the pain of change, think of what we will gain! We cannot afford to overlook the incredible cost of *not* changing.

Think about this in relation to our church life for a moment. The majority of the middle-to-older generation of people probably like things the way they are. They are pretty comfortable with the way in which they "do" church. But if we ignore the next generation of the Church and do not embrace the change that will release them into their destiny, we will be in big trouble. We will need to change some of our language, alter our methods of communication, modify our style of music and so on. Otherwise we could lose a whole generation from the Church. What a tragic loss that would be! The average congregational age of a growing church should be decreasing not increasing. The average age of our church members needs to be constantly falling if we are to keep growing to develop leaders for the future. Will we pay the price of change today so that we gain the prize of a better tomorrow? In order to do so, someone, somewhere, has to sacrifice their sentiments and traditions and prepare the way for the next season of the Church.

As we cooperate with this season of change, we discover that God is not sentimental and often has different priorities and agendas than we do. We often think the most change needs to start with one person or a specific area, but it often seems that God does not support our point of view as we find the spotlight turning on our own attitudes instead. Allowing the Holy Spirit to open up our hearts to a new season of change can be a dangerous journey!

I remember in the early 1990s I was attending a conference in Birmingham, U.K., and at the end of the morning session for leaders we began to pray. As we were praying, a man lay on the floor and began to cry out in a loud voice: "Clapham *Junction*, Clapham *Junction!*" and then he was silent. Having only returned from Africa a few months earlier, I was not even sure what or where Clapham Junction was. After a few whispered inquiries, I discovered that it was a large railway station in London. Still this prayer meant nothing to me, and I thought it rather odd until a few minutes later he began to shout again: "All change! All change!" I knew somehow this phrase had significance but still did not understand what was happening until a few weeks later when I was in London. I was attending a meeting in Earls Court, and on my way to the venue I had to change trains at Clapham Junction. As I approached the station I heard a man yelling, "All change! All change!" I attempted to get off the train and work my way across the platform, but the station was full of people, and so moving in any direction seemed impossible. After a few moments of pushing and shoving, I finally asked someone, "Is it always like this?" "Oh yes," she replied. "This is the place where everyone changes, and you have to know where you want to go and fight your way through the crowd to change trains. Otherwise you will just be left behind!" Her advice to me was, "Push and be determined or you will get lost in the crush!"

So I pushed and made my way to the next train and learned a lesson about "All change!" I discovered that with the spiritual, just as with the natural, change has the potential to be crushing, but if you are desperate and determined enough, you will start swimming upstream even if you are being pushed and pulled in the process. You have to doggedly stick to your chosen path if you are ever going to get to the right destination. Sometimes, just like salmon that swim against the flow and labor upstream when the season for fruitfulness is upon them, we have to work against the current, knowing that a season of change leading to fruitfulness requires cost and sacrifice. Once the salmon have given birth to their next generation, they die! Similarly, Hannah came from a family whose heritage was *double fruitfulness*, but it would only come out of a time of suffering. If we carry an ache for change and fruitfulness, then we must count the cost, be ready to be pushed and crushed, and walk the path of change.

## Choosing to live in the transition zone of change

So how do we navigate our way through a season of change? Once we have made the decision to live for change, then we have to have the courage to push through the transition time of uncertainty. It is not a comfortable feeling to leave the known and push out into uncharted territory with a dream of something new. But every pioneer has to pay a price for change. We have to be prepared for the fact that we will make mistakes. We need to be ready to adjust our worldviews and priorities. Change will cost us something. The most uncomfortable part of this season of change is living with the conflict of what you see in your spirit and what you actually see and have around you. Living in this contradiction between your reality and your vision takes courage and faith, but you need to learn to hold this in tension in the season of change.

Are you ready to move out into the land of adventure, where the horizon is blurred but the picture in your spirit is clearer? Are you ready to be a crazy person, ready to change the facts to align them with the truth of God's promises you are carrying in your spirit? Facts last for a day, but truth lasts for a lifetime. The facts can state that today you have no money in the bank to pay for these changes, but the truth of the Word of God tells you He will supply all your needs and give you the provision for this change. The facts can say that the X-ray you just had shows a cancer that will kill you or a womb that will never bear children, but the truth screams inside your being that you will be healed, that you will bear life. This is a dangerous journey—

one that requires courage, but one that we cannot afford to avoid walking any longer!

## Challenged to live in a season of change

A while ago one of my friends came and shared a prophetic picture that the Lord had given her specifically for me. My friend began, "I saw a picture of a lump of soft chewing gum. The gum was stuck down in one place, and then I watched as God's hand reached down and pulled on this lump of gum, stretching it to another place while part of the gum still remained tethered to its original spot. Rachel, God says that you are in a season of stretching, a season of transition. You will not be loosened from where you are rooted now, but God is going to stretch you into a new, deeper, hungrier place."

Just as a length of chewing gum tears if it is stretched too far, my friend went on to say that the only thing that would keep me from "breaking" during this period of transition was the discipline of being constantly lubricated by the grace of the Holy Spirit.

This picture became like a piece of grit in my spirit that caused me to start thinking, and then, over a period of time, God challenged me that there were a number of areas where He wanted to take the Church and stretch us. This is true for us corporately now. I believe God wants to stretch us from where we have been so comfortable into a new place of authority and destiny. I call these the *stretched-out zones*.

In the stretched-out zone we must remain malleable and ready for change so that God can use us. We must not become hard and brittle in our attitudes, like clay deprived of water. If we continue to walk in the grace of God, sustained by the power of the Holy Spirit, then even though we are being stretched, challenged and made to feel uncomfortable, we will be able to stay flexible and fluid, allowing God to mold and adapt us as He requires.

I was deeply moved by this word and it triggered a cry in my heart: *Oh God, help me! Please don't let me miss what You are doing because I am fearful of change. Please help me to cooperate with You in this season of transition.*

I believe that in these days there are many believers who are caught between two "seasons." Many are living in these stretched-out zones. In the stretched-out zone, you may be located in one place where you are quite happy, but suddenly you find that spiritually you are being pulled in an entirely different direction. Perhaps you have lived in your house for years; you love your community and the friendships you have; your children are happy in their school ... but suddenly you begin to feel these stretching pangs that disturb you, and you begin to wonder if it is time to move.

Obviously, living with this sense of change can fuel a deep frustration as we begin to feel uprooted for no apparent reason from what we know so well. Suddenly God begins to stretch our desire and create a hunger for a deeper knowledge of Him, and as a result the gap between our daily reality and the goal of our spiritual knowledge and hunger becomes unbearable. It is so frustrating to live with what you have when you know in your spirit that you should have so much more! But I believe that this is God's way of disturbing us from our spiritual comfort zones and challenging us to go deeper into Him and get ready to pay the price of change.

I believe that right now there are four areas in which God is deliberately challenging us, both as individuals and as churches, because He wants us to understand that He has so much more for us than we presently see. So where should we expect to feel the stretching pains?

## The stretched-out zones

### 1. Local church stretched into local community

At this time I believe that God wants us to change from having an inward-looking vision of local church to having a perspective that stretches the Church to partner with people in the local community. In other words, this is a time for the Church to go out rather than a time to sit and wait for the people to come in! Before anyone thinks I am dismissing the idea of local church, please let me explain: I love church! For many years we have spent much time teaching and training people how to become part of their local church. We have taught them how to behave, believe and belong, and we stressed the importance of their commitment to a local church. We have built church, pastored church, trained church, loved church; church has been our passion and our dream for a long time. We have focused on teaching people how to come *into* the church. Now God wants to show us how to *go out of* the church! Please do not misunderstand me. I am not saying that any of this process has been wrong. But a new time is upon us when God is stretching us to *move out* from our local church focus and have a new community focus. God is saying, "This is a change of season. No more training programs for you. Now I want your focus to be on your work colleagues, your neighbors, your community, your city. Lift up your eyes and look at the world outside your church doors."

Have you ever thought that your church is not as relevant to its surrounding community as it should be? Have you ever thought that if your church closed down, the community around you would barely even notice? Are you finding that at one time your faith seemed so much more relevant to others, but now it is becoming increasingly difficult for you to bridge the gap between church and community? If your answer is yes, then you are living in the stretched-out zone.

Of course, God has not *finished* with the Church. But He has not and never will finish with the world on our doorstep either! Over the last few years it has been important for us as believers to allow God to touch us inwardly. There has been so much pain and rejection in our own lives that it has been essential to spend some personal time alone with God, being healed. I believe this is why there has been such a strong theme of teaching, reminding the Church of the Father's heart and love, right across the world. First the Church needed to be healed so that it had a message for those outside its doors who also needed help. How can you minister to others what you have not experienced yourself? Emotional pain and rejection are as common in the world today as the common cold! But there is a reason why the Church needs to be healed quickly: so that we can get up and *go, go, go* to the lost of the world. If the Church does not go out into communities with this good news, then church becomes nothing more than a social club where we go to meet our friends. If that is all church has become, then we might as well go play golf on Sundays and get fit at the same time!

No, church has to become a *sending place* once again from where we *go out* to minister to the world. It must be stretched out from where it is in order to reach the place it needs to be to touch its community. Wherever I travel I meet people whose churches are entering this time of major transition. Why? Because God's hand is at work stretching us to where we should be. He is stretching us beyond the boundaries of nice, safe church. He is birthing in us a deep longing for harvest, a desire for change, a kind of divine frustration. If we resist this season of God's stretching, we could become cynical, rebellious or bitter, but I believe that as we cooperate with Him, He will ignite a fresh passion in us and give us a fresh vision for how His Kingdom can operate in our workplace, our neighborhood and all the "real" places of life.

So we need grace to embrace this transition, and we need to get ready for change. It is perhaps one of the toughest challenges that our church leaders face today. How do we turn an inward-looking church that is comfortable and inspire it to pay the price to go out and change the world? How do we train a people that have been used to the language "Come to church" to turn, go out of their secure environment with their testimonies and simply *be* church in the world? This is the challenge of the stretched-out zone!

## 2. Prayer or working for the harvest?

The second stretched-out zone that exists, and a zone in which I frequently find myself, is the old conflict of whether we should pray for the harvest or go out and work for the harvest. Most people around the world have identified me as an intercessor and a person who loves to pray, but recently a new passion is stirring deep within me that says, "Prayer is not enough; I must see souls saved!" Prayer, I have discovered, is merely the capital letter at the beginning of the sentence of history as far as God is concerned. Prayer is just a launchpad, a trigger point that starts a process. Prayer is the place where we connect with heaven and open the way so that something can begin to happen on earth. It is wonderful if we are praying for our neighbors, our work colleagues and our community, but this is not the end of the story; rather, it is just the first step. God wants us to go out and "write" the rest of the story with our lives. He is calling us to go out and to *do* the prayers of our hearts! In our church we often say, "Go talk to God about your neighbors, but then remember to talk to your neighbors about God!"

For too long, life in the Church has been about shutting the doors to the community and keeping all the believers inside caring for one another. Most of our resources and efforts have been spent on ourselves. Cocooned in the safety of our churches, we have fallen on our faces and prayed, done our forty days of intercession and spent time crying and groaning, but we have somehow still remained disconnected from real life. All this prayer has helped us to focus on Jesus, which is wonderful, but now it is time to stretch from this prayer place to see the faces of the harvest living all around us! God is stretching us in this zone from the altar of intimacy to the doorway of the community. Our hearts have to carry the burden for both the place of prayer and the place of evangelism.

When Jesus commissioned the seventy other disciples to go out and share the good news of the Gospel, He said these words: "The harvest truly is great, but the laborers are few; therefore pray the Lord of the harvest to send out laborers into His harvest" (Luke 10:2, NKJV).

Nothing has changed very much since Jesus spoke these words, as the Church still needs more workers who will go out and work. Prayer is good, but prayer is not enough—it is not the end of the story! Many intercessors have prayed for revival and the resulting harvest of souls but have then experienced a growing frustration as the answer to their prayers does not seem to satisfy them fully. I believe there is a godly frustration that is growing, stirred by the Holy Spirit who is saying, "Listen, I want to stretch your hearts and hands toward the harvest." Jesus said, "The harvest truly is great, but the laborers are few." So we see that the problem is not the *lack* of a harvest; the Bible assures us it is *great*. Our problem is that we cannot see this harvest and so are not motivated to *work* to bring it in. Some attitudes need to radically change in our lives so that once again there will be a Holy Spirit mass exodus from the Church into our neighborhoods and workplaces to win souls.

The exhortation of Joel 3:9–10 is a present-day challenge to us: "Proclaim this among the nations: Prepare for war! Rouse the warriors! Let all the fighting men draw near and attack. . . . Let the weakling say, 'I am strong!'"

Many intercessors have quoted this Scripture simply as a wake-up call for us to go to the place of prayer, but reading further into the text, why was the cry of warfare being stirred, and what was the focus of this urgent battle cry? Joel 3:14 tells us: "Multitudes, multitudes in the valley of decision! For the day of the LORD is near."

The mobilization of thousands of believers to prayer must now be directed toward bringing in a great harvest of souls because there are multitudes in the valley of decision—those who need to know God's mercy and grace. Instead of only rousing ourselves to warfare-like prayer, we now need to take the next step and continue to work until we see the harvest come. God wants to stretch our prayer lives into the harvest fields! It is time to pray like never before, and then stretch and change and work like never before, until we see the harvest reaped.

### 3. Prophetic vision versus reality

The third area in which I believe God is stretching His people is the area of balancing our prophetic vision against the reality of our lives. This is the zone of contradiction that contains the dichotomy between what you know and see in your spirit and your present reality. It is the tension between all the destiny and promises you carry in your heart—the potential of your life—in contrast to your experience in reality today. Many in the church carry a deep longing and yearning to see revival in their communities. They carry this desire deep inside themselves, and they believe that God will certainly bring it about. These believers have heard prophetic words about a coming revival, but they long to actually see what they know is written through the core of their beings.

Increasingly there is a frustration growing concerning these prophetic words. Many, including myself, have spoken out what we believe God is saying to His Church and calling her into, but we are tired of waiting; we want to see it! We are in a stretched-out time zone between the speaking of these prophetic promises and the implementation and outworking of them in our world.

Many prophetic people have this frustration that cries out, "God, please let Your Kingdom come! Let Your will be done *now* in this place." We have a Jacob-type wrestling in our heart that says, "I am sick and tired of being promised something tomorrow. It has to be today! I am wrestling because, God, You've so stirred my hunger, You've so stirred my passion, that I can't be satisfied with anything else. God, You have to complete Your words for me! I don't want just more prophetic signs and promises; I want to see You in Your power in my community! God, please satisfy me!"

I want to encourage you to let this cry be stirred even if it is uncomfortable. Do not let this cry be stifled! Some people have grown weary and even cynical in this place of stretching and now respond, when challenged, with the familiar cliché, "Been there, done that, got the T-shirt!" We have almost convinced ourselves that being aware of the concept is the same as having the answer. But we have not "done that" completely yet, and we do *not* have the T-shirt in our hands! As yet we still have only the vision. It is so easy to deny the reality of what we *actually have* and get caught up in the prophetic excitement of our promises. But let God stretch you to face reality and stir again the desire to see all your promises birthed.

In Romans 4:19–20 we read these extremely challenging words about Abraham: "Without weakening in his faith, he faced the fact that his body was as good as dead. . . . Yet he did not waver through unbelief regarding the promise of God. . . ."

Abraham considered the facts about his body and its potential for successfully fathering a child. Naturally speaking, he knew the situation was hopeless, and yet he accepted that God had spoken and declared that he would be the father of many nations! Abraham looked the facts squarely in the face, but he did not resort to unbelief. He believed that, despite the bleak outlook, God was able. We need to do the same. Take a hard look at the facts of your life and start saying, "Yes, but I know God is able!"

I believe the days are fast approaching when we will say, like Simeon and Anna, the prophetic people who frequented the temple looking for a Savior: "Now my eyes have seen!" But we need to endure this stretched-out zone and believe for the change in which our dreams and visions will become a reality that we can touch and handle. Soon these days will come, and we will watch God fulfill His word over our lives and nations. So get ready for change!

### 4. Intimacy versus power

This fourth and final stretched-out zone is probably the most uncomfortable contradiction: the expanse that exists between our knowledge of intimacy with God and our experience of His power. We know that this needs to change, and we are increasingly aware of the necessity of balance in this area of our lives.

Over these past few years we have seen a new level of awareness in the Church regarding the need for, and the possibility of, intimacy with the Father. For many, it has been the first time they have come to understand and know God as a true father figure. More than that, many have had the revelation of God as our loving Daddy who longs to spend time with us face-to-face. But while this understanding of intimacy and friendship with God has been vital, I believe God is now stretching us again and calling us to a new level of relationship with Him. This will require more change and will shake us out of the secure comfort of time alone with Daddy, placing us in a wilderness where we will learn to work with the God of power. This shift will feel like a major culture shock for many, but we must remember that it was in this place of wilderness that Jesus had spiritual encounters that transformed Him and enabled Him to emerge with the power of the Spirit on His life. In the same way, God can touch our lives and stretch us in new and dynamic ways when we learn to walk in the wilderness.

The wilderness can be a lonely place for sure—a place where we feel cut off from all our normal support mechanisms of friendships and relationships—but it is the place where we are utterly dependent on God and He gains our undivided attention. In the intimate place, we come to know the fatherhood of God and learn to feel His endless love, but in the desert place we need to encounter the power of God and the fight of faith. In Scripture, every person who went through a wilderness season emerged from the experience having been empowered by God.

The journey of God's stretching times can seem strange and disorientating. There are times when you feel like you are learning in both places at once! You are aware of your intimacy with the Father, and yet you also know the isolation and preparation that must take place for His power to come in the desert. At these times pray, "God, give me the grace to be stretched. God, help me change. Let me learn more about Your fatherhood and the place of intimacy, but also teach me more about Your anointing and power and the battle of faith."

Yes, intimacy with God is wonderful, but we cannot stay reveling in His presence when there are so many other lives that still need His touch. We also need to be the instruments of His power so He can use us to touch and change people's lives!

In this stretched-out zone, God stirs in us a passion for His presence and anoints us with the power of the Spirit so we will be more effective for His service in a ministry of the miraculous. We need to be a people who are flexible and can quickly change our focus. We need to be fulfilled and satisfied in His presence but also ready to go out and change our world as we carry His power and see miracles.

## Three things that happen during the stretched-out zone

I believe many readers will recognize these stretched-out zones and be able to testify that they are living in one or more of them at the moment. The areas that I have mentioned are: the longing to be in the local church versus the desire to move beyond church and touch the community; the calling for the place of prayer and intercession versus a longing to go and work among the harvest; our sense of destiny and prophetic promises versus the need to see them working in everyday life; and the challenge between knowing His face and carrying His power.

Now I want to focus on what happens during that time of stretching. Most of us recognize that we need to change as we grow in our relationship with God, but I am sure many still struggle with the question, "Yes, but why must the season of change stretch us and be uncomfortable?"

Simply put, God has to stretch us because usually we are reluctant to embrace change, especially when we have become comfortable with our present circumstances. God has to disturb our comfort zones and remove the feathers from our nests to cause us to move. Furthermore, God has to irritate and awaken new desires in us so He can redefine our understanding and bring the passion of our lives more into line with His thinking and desires.

I believe there are three main characteristics of this stretching season that are important for us to understand.

### 1. Stretching is a time of TRANSFORMATION

Whether God is stretching us as individuals or corporately, such as in our church, this process is all about transformation. It is literally a time of metamorphosis. There are several scriptures where God talks about changing, forming or making us, and each time the Greek root word is *metamorpheo*:

> And we, who with unveiled faces all reflect the Lord's glory, are being *transformed* [*metamorpheo*] into his likeness with ever-increasing glory, which comes from the Lord, who is the Spirit.
>
> 2 Corinthians 3:18, emphasis added

> Do not conform any longer to the pattern of this world, but be *transformed* [*metamorpheo*] by the renewing of your mind. Then you will be able to test and approve what God's will is—his good, pleasing and perfect will.
>
> Romans 12:2, emphasis added

The full force of *metamorpheo* becomes apparent when we watch the process of change in the insect world. Insects are creatures that start life living in one dimension. They are earthbound, and then they go through an incredible process of change called metamorphosis in order to reach maturity and their full potential. They begin as larvae, develop into pupae and eventually reach adulthood in an entirely different form. The example we all know best is that of the caterpillar turning into a butterfly. This insect is born to fly, but it starts life crawling on the earth, and after a process of change, struggle and what looks like death, it emerges transformed with new colors and able to fly. This is the kind of metamorphosis of which the Bible speaks.

I believe we have the wrong picture about the method God uses to change us. The Bible makes it clear that, as believers, we are engaged in a process that will see us transformed from one degree of glory to the next. But somehow we view this journey as God simply improving and refining what we already are. Let me use another illustration. Many people view this process of change like a balloon being filled with air. As God progressively fills us with His power, we just expand and change size, but we are still essentially the same balloon, retaining more or less the same features and abilities. I do not believe that's what God does at all! No, God wants us to undergo a major transformation just like the caterpillar! A caterpillar can only walk on the ground and exist in that dimension, but a butterfly flies free and is able to move in two completely different dimensions—on the earth and in the air! God wants us to know this transformation, too. Where we have been tethered to a fixed dimension and so limited in our power and experience, He wants us to fly free and know radical change and freedom in our lives. This is how different God wants us to be from how we are now.

If we want to move from being totally church-focused to being relevant to our communities, then it will take more than just a few minor adjustments. It will require a major transformation of our hearts and then our actions and priorities. If we want to move from being just in our prayer closets to the harvest field, that will require a major transformation in the way we organize our lives and friendships.

Perhaps the most sobering part is this: Transformation requires us to be prepared to die! If you want to see God break through in an unprecedented way in your life, then you have to be prepared to get into the chrysalis and be radically changed. It means having to give up all that you were before. It means you have to stop and allow a time of change to be worked through your life. It is not going to always feel nice, but the reward of this change makes the cost worthwhile, for you will find that all you have ever dreamed of will be brought to life by God during this season of change! You have to be prepared to shun the fear of losing the familiar and step out into the unknown. Before, you were walking on the ground, feeding on leaves. Now, you are flying through the air and feeding on pollen—total transformation! He makes all things new. You are a new creation—the old has gone and the new has come!

## 2. It is a time of TRANSITION

God's stretching process is also a time of transition, a journey from one state of being or place to another. Giving birth is the best picture I can think of to illustrate this transition time. Most women who have given birth will remember that moment when suddenly your body is consumed with a strong desire to push, and yet the doctor calmly states, "Just hold on, you are in transition stage. Don't push yet." She will make you hold and keep holding until the moment to push is right. In this transition phase, circumstances are beyond your control. All you can do is listen and obey the instructions. You hold when you're told to hold and push when you're told to push!

There is basically nothing you can do to make yourself the butterfly that the Holy Spirit designed you to be. All you can do is hold. It is chrysalis time. Just be sure that you "hold" in God's presence and do not become cynical because the process seems to be taking a long time. Do not try to run away from the process, either. Just trust God that, in due course, this time of concealment will give way to a time of revelation.

God will invariably use this chrysalis time to work in you and will challenge and shape your character. It is not a comfortable time, because you are a captive waiting for this transition and transformation to come to fruition, but it is now that God can work most effectively. So let the butterflies of the next season come forth—each person with his or her colors and style designed by God. But remember, if you touch a butterfly as it is emerging from its chrysalis, you will damage the wings and it will never fly. This is a season of isolation when you need to wrestle and struggle with the various issues and let them do their work in your life. Then when the season has finished, the very wrestle of faith will have formed your wings so you will fly!

What kind of things will God do with us during the journey of transition? I believe there are at least four:

i. During this time God will cause you to assess every priority and agenda. He will cause you to ask yourself, "What is my motivation for the things I am involved with?" It is a time when God will cause you to look soberly at who you are and why you do the things you do.

ii. It is a time when God will show you how much you need His grace in your life. During my own chrysalis times I have come to realize that apart from God I have absolutely nothing! God has not allowed me to be crushed, but I have come to realize afresh the awesomeness of God and the smallness of who I am by comparison. You may never feel more vulnerable than in this chrysalis season, but God will help you to understand how sufficient His grace is for you.

iii. It is a time when God will get you back to basics. In the chrysalis, your prayers, rather than becoming more sophisticated, will "grow" down instead of up! God will take you back to basic, foundational truths, upon which your life must be built. God will also ask you some nitty-gritty questions about your life. What is your marriage really like? How close to Him are you living day to day? God wants you to get real about the basic building blocks that really matter.

iv. It is a time when God will give you an obedience check. <u>Are you doing the important things that the Bible instructs</u> you to do? Are you living according to His commands? Are you being trustworthy in small things so that God can bless you with greater things to do for Him? Are you living to please Jesus or to please yourself?

### 3. It is a time for a DIFFERENT SEASON

It is important that we realize God is stretching us because it is time to move into a different season. The old paradigm must pass away because a new one is emerging. We need to realize that change has a purpose in the Kingdom of God and does not happen just because God likes watching us to see how we handle it. <u>I believe that all the stretching we are experiencing in</u> <u>the Church and in our lives at the moment has a Kingdom</u> <u>purpose for our nations</u>. God is about a higher purpose than we can immediately perceive. He is ushering in a new season of effectiveness in His Body, the Church, and He is challenging us to move into this new day with Him. So will we change? This change does have a cost, so will we be people of courage and pay the price to go through this season of transition to give birth to the new era of the Church? Will we train up the next generation in tradition or allow them to run their race with their distinctive, releasing to them the blessing of our wisdom? In the next chapter we will examine the challenge this heart of change will bring as we begin to mentor and train the next generation.

# The Movement for Change

**3**

> "It takes a lot of courage to release the familiar
> and seemingly secure, to embrace the new.
> But there is no real security in what is no longer meaningful.
> There is more security in the adventurous
> and exciting, for in movement there is life,
> and in change there is power."
> —Alan Cohen

In the last chapter we discussed the cost of change and realized it is a price we must pay if we are ever going to see our dreams become a reality. Unfortunately, change always requires us to let go of what we know before we can have the new. In fact, often we have to let go in order to *grow into* the new; it does not always come immediately. One thing is sure: We cannot keep doing the same things and expect different results; we need to let the process of change accelerate us into a new season of breakthrough.

In Leviticus 26 we discover that God wants us to let go in every area of our lives. Here we read,

"I will look on you with favor and make you fruitful and
increase your numbers, and I will keep my covenant with you.
You will still be eating last year's harvest *when you will have to
move it out to make room for the new."*

verses 9–10, emphasis added

God touches even the good harvest in our lives and asks us to
move it out of the central position it occupies to make room for
the new. In practice this means that when the season of change
is upon us, sometimes we have to let go of the good experiences
we've had, alter close relationships and form new ones, change
the way we do things and even end activities that have been
useful until now.

In spiritual terms, sadly it is often those at the forefront of the
last move of God who are the first to oppose the next move of
God. This goes against God's character, as He is always doing
something new. The bottom line is, we must always stay
flexible. God is not sentimental and often the things that are
very important to us do not seem to be so critical to Him. We
must let God build His Church and also make any alterations
He desires!

One day when I was considering some major changes that
were happening in my church (and feeling quite upset about
them), God gave me this picture: I saw the scene of an old-
fashioned orchard contained by a high stone wall. The trees
were mature and planted quite closely together. It was late
fall, the trees were beginning to lose their leaves and some of
the last apples and pears were still on the branches. As I was
watching this scene, looking at this mature and fruitful orchard,
suddenly a huge mechanical digger appeared! Next it lowered
its front bucket over the nice stone orchard wall and began
digging and lifting up mature trees out of the orchard and
moving them to a totally different place. My first reaction was

horror as I looked at the mess it was making of this perfect orchard! But then I felt God say to me, "Get ready for change. I am going to relocate mature people; I am going to pick up fruitful trees and move them. It is time for Me to redistribute My assets to allow room for a new season of rapid growth."

I believe this is a season when, just like a deck of cards, God will shuffle His pack. He is bringing different streams together and allowing a new cross-pollination and blending of our gifts and styles. In the natural, cross-pollination increases fruitfulness as the new diversity and combination of DNA increases fertility. As in the natural, so in the spiritual. I believe God will use this time to broaden our horizons and challenge our mindsets. As these different rivers begin to flow together, there will be a new sound in the land, and change will be in the air!

As this season of change continued in our church, I found that again and again God would reassure me with pictures to explain what was happening. Another day when I was praying, I had a picture of different groups of ducks, each group in its own backyard, swimming in its own little pond. I was watching these ponds from an aerial position when suddenly I saw a flood coming, and the water level rose dramatically. Suddenly, the boundaries of these little ponds got lost in the bigger flood, and all the ducks began to swim together in a bigger place. God said to me, *It is time to move from a pond-like mentality that is limited, to a broader lake mentality where many different species live and swim together. This is what My Kingdom is like.*

During this season of change in my life, I went to visit an exhibition in a national park while on vacation. As I entered the building a large sign stated, FOREST FIRES—FRIEND OR FOE? I sensed God speak to me and challenge me to learn about these trees so that I could understand the season of change in the church. A further sign boldly stated, <u>FIRE—THE FRIEND OF THE NEXT GENERATION</u>! The exhibition concluded that forest fires are the friend of the next generation because without fire there is never room for any new growth. In most forests, the skyline gets so choked with the foliage of the mature trees that smaller trees cannot reach toward the light and grow. It is only when the heat of the fire comes and thins the trees that there is space for growth. It is also the heat of the fire that triggers the germination of dormant seeds that have lain on the forest floor for so long.

I believe this is the same in the Church. When hot fires and trials come, and mature people move and others get scattered, this provides an opportunity for new people to grow and function.

Life always brings change! God made it that way. He is living, active and moving. The only things that do not change or move are *dead things*. Leviticus 26 challenges us to keep moving, to keep putting aside the old and embracing the new, to not get stuck in one season.

## The season of transfer

In addition to staying flexible and being prepared for change at all times, I believe it is critical for the Church to understand it is in a permanent season of *transfer*. By this I mean the transfer of wisdom, skill and anointing from one generation to the next. There is nothing more crucial for the Church of today to grasp if the Church of tomorrow is to be blessed and released into its fullness. We need to pay the price of mentoring and giving our life for others, to grow and train the future leaders in our ranks. It is a season in which we need to see three generations working together (just as God has always referred to Himself as the God of Abraham, Isaac and Jacob; He holds three generations in His name). So we need to be prepared to be spiritual midwives, not just spiritual parents! What does this mean? To help birth other people's dreams in God, not just our own. The bride of intimacy now needs to become the mother of influence and teach the next generation. This is the day for us to be role models and heroes, so that our spiritual children will have dreams and aspirations. Like Paul we should be challenging our Timothys and provoking them to follow our lives as we follow Jesus. This needs to be the day of fathers and mothers working together for the next generation.

Generational transfer is something that even the world understands but often fails to negotiate successfully. You can see it happen in companies when there is a change of leadership after a long period of stability. Sometimes, if the former leader was effective in his or her role, the reconstituted board, the staff and the organization as a whole will continue to work perfectly, and the transfer is easy. But many times when the successor takes over, there are difficulties, especially when it is a father and son in a family-run business. Often in these situations the son has not been trained adequately to fill his father's shoes, so insecurities and tensions arise in the company. But where there is a good relationship between the father and his son, and people know there is a secure bond, there is an easy transfer.

Generally, in our society today we are losing our respect for the older generation, and people do not give them any credit for their wisdom. There has been a breakdown of trust and relationships, and a gulf has developed. Age does not gain respect anymore. Yet in Scripture we clearly find the principle that we are required to honor our father and mother. In fact, that is mentioned five times in the New Testament alone. Why is this connection so important? We need to understand that where there is no covenantal connection of relationship, there can be no transfer of wisdom, and it is a sad thing to lose all that the previous generation learned. If you want to receive a generational blessing, you have to have a generational relationship. As we consider this movement of change and our responsibility to train and release the next generation, let us look more closely at the story of Ruth and Naomi and find the keys of wisdom for us today.

## The book of Ruth—or should it be Naomi?

I have always considered the life of Ruth to be the focal point of the book of Ruth in the Bible; after all, it is named after her! But recently, as I read the book again, I was struck by the essential influence of Naomi throughout the book. As I examined the life of Naomi and the vital mentoring role she adopted, I wondered whether it should really be called the book of Naomi! Ruth found her rightful place because of the strength and wisdom of Naomi. This book is the story of a successful partnership between a mother-in-law and a daughter-in-law—two women who both found satisfaction and fulfilled their destiny when they committed to a covenantal relationship. Such generational relationships are vital for us today if we are to truly fulfil our purpose for God. Women need other women to inspire them, and men need strong male friendships to stimulate them.

If we are to see this movement of change result in the strengthening of the next generation, then we must examine the whole area of trust. For many of us, trust issues have become the major hindrance to our having good relationships. Mothers and fathers have not fulfilled their roles as encouragers and friends, so we have felt rejected; churches have had splits and leadership difficulties, so we have felt confused; friends have betrayed our confidence, so we have felt vulnerable and ashamed; prayer partnerships that we believed in and shared together in have become fragmented, so life relationships are lost. As a result our ability to trust others has suffered greatly.

As we turn to the book of Ruth we recognize something of

this issue in the relationships it describes. Chapter 1 tells us that Naomi, Ruth and Orpah were living through a difficult season in their nation and in their personal lives. Naomi had been through a time of famine and difficulty and had had to move to another nation. Then her two sons had met and married Moabite women. Now they were all in a new season of difficulty, as both her sons and Naomi's husband had died and there were no grandchildren. These women were all alone. In Ruth 1:8 we read Naomi's response as her daughters-in-law try to comfort and remain with her: "Go back, each of you, to your mother's home. May the LORD show kindness to you, as you have shown to your dead and to me."

Naomi's response is the natural response of a grieving wife and mother. Here is a wounded, hurting woman who has just been through the trauma of loss, and she has nothing left for these women. All she wants to do is to find a place for herself and detach her life from her daughters-in-law. Like us, her natural instinct after a time of difficulty is to isolate, withdraw and find space to recover. You can almost hear her cry, "Just leave me alone. Go away. I need time for me." But we discover that at least one of the women is not so easily persuaded: We read in verse 14 that while Orpah left, Ruth clung to Naomi. Ruth had decided this was just one relationship too many to lose, and she would not let Naomi go. Naomi felt she no longer had anything she could contribute to the relationship, so she wanted out, but verse 16 recounts for us Ruth's famous statement of commitment: "Don't urge me to leave you or to turn back from you. Where you go I will go, and where you stay I will stay. Your people will be my people and your God my God."

Ruth is determined to stay linked and in a relationship with Naomi. The Bible then tells us that once Naomi realized Ruth was determined to stay, she stopped urging her to leave. This decision of commitment changed the direction of not only

Ruth's life but also Naomi's. They both embarked on a journey of change. Naomi had been living in Moab, representing a backslidden place. It was not the land of her God, but now she joined with Ruth, and they returned to the House of Bread, Bethlehem, together. Naomi still had emotional needs and was not very easy to be with. She instructed the people of Bethlehem, "Don't call me Naomi [meaning pleasant and bountiful]. . . . Call me Mara [meaning bitter]" (verse 20). But once back in Bethlehem Naomi rediscovered her roots; she found her family again, and this awakened her dreams and destiny. Suddenly Naomi was no longer pushing Ruth away; she changed and began pushing Ruth into her destiny, caring for her and instructing her.

As Naomi began to serve the next generation, she started to find great fulfillment in her own life. She found hope again. As she served Ruth, she found that her needs were met, too, and her whole perspective changed. A similar set of circumstances are challenging us today as we seek to see change. You meet many of the older generation who feel they have been over-looked and their hopes have been disappointed. As the next generation begins to emerge and presses into their space with all their plans and dreams, the older generation can sound bitter and withholding rather than enthusiastic. You may hear this type of conversation around you: "No one helped us to fulfill our dreams." "I need to have my chance first." "I'm too busy doing what I need to do. I have dreams, too. You sort out your own problems!" We see Naomi's *initial* attitude mirrored in churches across our land as we see the hopes, dreams and aspirations of generational relationships being pushed away, the older generation tending to withhold friendship and wisdom instead of giving it. When this happens, we leave the Ruths of today abandoned and confused. We need to let the next generation connect with us and run with us. This is not a time to get bitter. Rather, we must allow a better attitude to grip us; we must change and help the next generation to break through.

The end of the book of Ruth provides us with the best picture of all. In Ruth 4:17 we find Naomi sitting with a son again! I love this picture, and I can just imagine the scene: Here is Naomi, looking older, but with her face glowing with pride. In her arms she holds her dream—a grandchild. She had thought this could never happen. After all, her husband is dead and both her sons are dead; how could she ever have a grandchild? But, because she allowed Ruth into her life, she is now able to sit on her porch in her rocking chair, singing gently as she gazes into the face of her little child. The whole neighborhood is excited, and the story is out: "Have you seen? Naomi has a SON!" (see Ruth 4:17). By serving the next generation, Naomi found that her dreams came true.

Naomi discovered that her destiny as a woman was to work with the next generation. I believe each of us will eventually come into a season in our lives when we have that same responsibility. It has nothing to do with our natural situation, whether we have children or not. This is a spiritual calling. There is an anointing on the Church to train, release and nurture the children of tomorrow. Even if you do not feel naturally "parental," there is nothing to stop you from influencing others' lives and helping them to find their dream and destiny. This is a time when everyone needs to reach one, and then teach one to reach one! It is time to touch the lives of others and bring change. We must be the carriers of hope to the hopeless. This is not about our age in the natural, but about our experience in God.

## Mentors for times of change

Like Naomi, we must help the next generation walk through their difficult times. Sometimes there will be times of death, spiritually if not literally. Knowing how to navigate such times can release a fragrance that will increase their anointing to serve the generation that follows them. Inevitably opposition and trials come, but we can teach our Ruths how to stand strong, even in the tough times. We know that even in the desperate times, there is a joy to be found that can change our outlook and enable us to break through and birth our dreams, but those experiencing hardship for the first time need an experienced coach to cheer them on! We need to encourage the next generation to make the right and sometimes hard choices and to keep moving forward even in the difficult times.

We see this pattern in the life of Esther. Esther was a commoner with no royal background or training, naive with regard to the protocols, procedures and expectations of being a queen. Yet here she was, an immigrant in a foreign land, about to be married to the king! Esther needed the practical wisdom of her uncle Mordecai, and the guidance of the eunuch Hegai to help her make wise choices. Her training took time, but eventually she emerged ready to understand and engage in her purpose in God.

This is an Esther hour for our nations. Many have been born for this season and have a purpose for this hour. We need to connect with the next generation and help them walk the corridors of power and bring change. In previous revivals, men, women and young people carried a "reformers" anointing. The Holy Spirit urged them onto the streets, into the prisons and into the places of power to change the face of their communities. We need to identify and release those with a similar Esther anointing, while others of us function like Mordecai and Hegai, being prepared to stay in the background to guide and advise those who have been given the places of influence.

Several years ago my passion for mentoring began in earnest. I suddenly realized that there are certain results you can produce in conferences of thousands of people, in churches of hundreds or with leaders' groups of fifties, but there is something unique that can happen in small groups of tens in which you share your life. I also noticed that when some leaders die, they leave an incredible legacy, their team continues secure and the vision keeps pressing forward. But when other leaders die, it seems that their vision and resources disappear very quickly. I realized that it will always be people, not paper, videos or organizations, that will carry the vision from generation to generation.

Jesus modeled this in His own life. He preached to thousands and had many followers, but He lived with twelve men, and they were His disciples. It was these twelve who carried on the vision after His death. I felt God challenge me to look at the role of the mentor/trainer/teacher and to copy the example of the Holy Spirit, our spiritual mentor—the One who comes alongside us and helps us to adapt and change in order to fulfill our destiny. We, too, need to be facilitators of change. With the fragmentation of family life and with moral and ethical standards disappearing, we need to personally train the next generation so they have a correct value system. Many of the next generation have never had their consciences trained, and we need to work with them so they can recognize the truth. As attitudes of godlessness in our society are constantly increasing, we need to work with the next generation and help them start a movement for change in the opposite direction. We need to be mentors who will love and help the children and youth in this day and age. *This is the time to touch the next generation.* We must turn our hearts to one another and close the generation gap and care for one another.

If there is no generational *connection*, there will be no generational *transfer*. There must be a real relational and committed contact between spiritual parents and children so that the distilled wisdom of the former can be imparted to the latter. As we read in Luke 1, this connection is one of the necessary conditions to prepare the way for God to come:

> "And he will go on before the Lord, in the spirit and power of Elijah, *to turn the hearts of the fathers to their children and the disobedient to the wisdom of the righteous*—to make ready a people prepared for the Lord."
>
> Luke 1:17, emphasis added

So let us turn our hearts to one another and be flexible as we start a movement for change. Let us take our responsibility to nurture and help release the dreams of others who desire to be a force for change in God's Kingdom.

# SECTION 2

*Learning to Carry Your Dreams*

# You Were Born to Dream

## 4

*"All people dream, but not equally. Those who dream*
*by night in the dusty recesses of their mind,*
*wake in the morning to find that it was vanity.*
*But the dreamers of the day are dangerous people,*
*for they dream their dreams with open eyes,*
*and make them come true."*

—T. E. Lawrence (aka Lawrence of Arabia)

## Time to awaken the dreamer

One morning as I was waking up, I felt God speak to me as follows: *Rachel, can you see the roses in the wilderness before they bloom? Can you see the bright light in the city or only the gross darkness of people's sin? Can you see hope or only the pain on their faces? Can you see an army that marches triumphantly or just a valley of dry bones? Rachel, what can you see? Can you dream?* As I shook myself fully awake, I realized that God was speaking to me about changing the focus of my vision. I was always looking at the facts and making my assessment, but God wanted me to look beyond what I could see naturally and perceive spiritually what He was doing in the secret place.

We are always being confronted by statistics and facts on the one hand and prophetic promises of change on the other. Unfortunately, there seems to be a growing gap between the facts as we know them and the truth of the promises of God. So what do we see? Can we believe in faith to see disasters turn to victories? Can we see the doctor's report diagnosing terminal cancer turn into life? Can we turn the evidence of a broken marriage into a healed relationship? Can we see beyond the facts and hold fast to the truth of God? We need to begin to hear the voice of God and dream with Him, so that in the place of prayer we can turn the facts into breakthrough. But someone has to dream that life can be different. Someone has to see in the Spirit that breakthrough can come. Someone has to be the vessel of God and allow the prophetic word, the dream, to be incubated inside them. Someone has to see the invisible and dream of the impossible with God.

We have been created by God with a capacity to dream. We were born to see beyond our natural reality and understand the spiritual destiny to come. In the following passage we read, "We fix our eyes not on what is seen, but on what is unseen. For what is seen is temporary, but what is unseen is eternal" (2 Corinthians 4:18).

We need to fix our eyes on our spiritual destiny again. It is time to realize that the facts of today are only temporary, but our eternal destiny will last forever. What God has said will be accomplished, and now we must dream with Him and allow His breath to stir our prophetic vision once again. This is the time for the Church in our nation to breathe again and awaken hope and expectation.

A quote by William J. Clinton challenged me recently: "When our memories outweigh our dreams, we have grown old." Unfortunately, much of the Church has "grown old" in its mentality, and it lives in the memory of the last great revivals. We recount the stories of yesterday but have lost the hope that we can write the story of today. We must begin to *live* the dreams given to us by God, not just record them. Recently, the Holy Spirit challenged me, *Rachel, do not just* journal *your dreams—be the dream.* We must look at how we process the expectations we have carried and the visions of tomorrow that we long for, and fulfill the dreams of God with our lives in this hour. We must listen to the trumpet of hope that is sounding across the nation and ask again for a stirring of the image of our big God, who can do all that He has promised to do.

## Dare to dream

Dreaming is part of our spiritual nature because it is a part of the very nature of God. Before God created the world and everything we see today, He dreamed of it. He saw it in His mind's eye before speaking it into being. God has created us to be like Him, so when the Holy Spirit comes upon us we begin to dream. Joel 2:28–29 says,

> "And afterward,
>     I will pour out my Spirit on all people.
> Your sons and daughters will prophesy,
>     your old men will dream dreams,
>     your young men will see visions.
> Even on my servants, both men and women,
>     I will pour out my Spirit in those days."

As soon as the Holy Spirit comes upon people, they begin to prophesy and dream! What is prophecy? One of my simple definitions is "declaring the dream of God." When we prophesy, we are declaring God's dream for a person or a circumstance. We are speaking out what God has already destined and planned for an individual life or nation and so are publicly declaring the dream of God for that situation.

There are certain environments in which we often find we can hear the voice of God more clearly and begin to feel a rising hope, a new sense of expectation and an ability to see and dream of the future. Usually this happens when we are in a place where we can feel the Holy Spirit. When the Spirit comes upon us, we begin to dream, and vision is conceived in our spirit man. Like Mary, when God speaks to us and the Holy Spirit broods over our lives, we get pregnant with the destiny and purpose of God. Once we receive a specific word from God that He is going to do something in or through us, we need to remember that most dreams take a lifetime to fulfill. Many of us are fearful of letting our dream nature be expressed. We are afraid that we will be misunderstood or crushed. If you have ever felt that way, let the Holy Spirit blow on your life again. Dare to dream! Dare to dream that *you* can be an instrument of change, that God can use *you* as part of His movement for change.

## Discovering the dream of God for you

When God created us, He had a vision for our lives. None of us are accidents; we are specifically designed for a purpose and created to be able to fulfill the dream of God for our lives. Jeremiah 1:5–8 makes this clear:

> "Before I formed you in the womb I knew you,
>     before you were born I set you apart;
>     I appointed you as a prophet to the nations."
>
> "Ah, Sovereign LORD," I said, "I do not know how to speak;
> I am only a child."

But the LORD said to me, "Do not say, 'I am only a child.' You must go to everyone I send you to and say whatever I command you. Do not be afraid of them, for I am with you and will rescue you," declares the LORD.

God created you with his GOD-DNA inside you! You were created with a God-given destiny and purpose in mind, and your physical, natural and spiritual gifts were provided to fulfill the dream. Before we were even born, God knew the details and the depths of our personalities. He knew our race, our culture, our intellect, our gender and our destiny. None of this shocks God. He knew our weaknesses and our strengths. He knew everything and still loved us! You were formed by God and set apart for a purpose; you were appointed and then born! God had already seeded His call on your life in your spiritual DNA. You were part of His dream from the moment you were born. When we choose to connect with God and give Him our lives, He breathes upon us and activates this hidden call. Now we have to work with the Spirit to activate it fully.

## Know you have a destiny

Jeremiah 20:9 speaks of the "hidden" call of God inside us: "But if I say, 'I will not mention him or speak any more in his name,' *his word is in my heart like a fire*, a fire shut up in my bones. I am weary of holding it in; indeed, I cannot" (emphasis added).

Each one of us is created with a specific "destiny word" from God hidden in our bones, and to live satisfied we need to fulfill this word. But there is often a struggle for this word of God to be revealed and become fleshed out in our lives. We read of Jesus in John 1:14 that "the Word became flesh and made His dwelling among us." Just as Jesus had to walk through a process to live out God's dream for Him in the flesh, so that must be true for each of our lives. The word of God hidden in our bones must be lived! Otherwise we will grow weary of holding it inside.

Each person then has to discover the mission statement God has written into our DNA. What is the mandate, the assignment, specific to us? How do we know what our call is? If you are struggling with this, ask yourself these questions:

1. What really matters to me?
2. What do I live for?
3. What motivates me and makes me passionate?
4. What legacy do I want to leave behind for others?

The answers to these questions will reveal the core cry of your dreams and help you identify your call. The goal of your life should be to ensure that the main thing you are doing is aligned to the main passion of your life.

Once we have identified the word that is shut up in our bones, we must understand that we will never feel truly fulfilled unless we obey this call. I believe God will judge us not on what we did or did not do per se, but on what we did compared to what we were called to do for the Kingdom.

In this hour God is calling us to take our place and be vessels who dream of change and then workers in the Kingdom who bring change. We must do what the Holy Spirit is telling us to do on the inside of our beings. It will be a test of obedience. Usually the actions of obedience are not convenient. Recently, Gordon and I spent some time assessing what we were doing with our lives. When we considered the above questions, we realized that we loved the local church and loved students and youth. We had a passion to see them trained and released. But what we were doing at that time in our lives did not really satisfy this cry, and we felt God challenge us to move. This was not convenient, as it meant we had to sell our family home, find new office space and distance ourselves from long-term relationships. This was hard, but for the sake of the call we had to obey and move. We realized that the fingerprints of God on the inside of our beings meant we were compelled to obey the call. It may not always be convenient, and sometimes it will not make much sense, but we have to go!

## Deal with the reasons you hesitate

As we begin to recognize the destiny of God on our lives and know we should be part of this process of change, suddenly all the legitimate reasons why God could never use us seem to surface. If we look at the call of Jeremiah again, we can recognize this pattern: "I do not know how to speak; I am only a child."

As we recognize God's call on us and begin to understand our identity in Christ, there will always be "buts": "But, Lord, surely you know that I'm like this . . . ?" Jeremiah focused on his youth and his lack of experience as a public speaker as an excuse for not responding to God's call. We use similar arguments: "I'm not experienced enough." "I've got small children to look after at the moment." "I don't know God well enough yet to do that."

From a young age I always admired preachers, and at times I would sit and imagine that I was on the platform preaching to thousands. But as I grew up I realized that these dreams were unreasonable. After all, I was a woman, and "women do not preach." So I used my gender as an excuse every time I felt God challenge me to step out and speak. The conversations in my head were endless: *God, don't You know I am a woman? I cannot do this!* After many such statements, one day God replied, *Rachel, when will you realize that I made you with your call, which I*

*put into a female body? I am not confused; just obey Me!* We will
always have genuine reasons that make our hesitations seem
plausible, but we need to embrace the call and just do what He
asks us to do.

I discovered a long time ago that God does not want our
abilities, just our availability. He does not need our experience,
just our obedience. God can use us if we will untangle our lives
from all our excuses. He is looking for willing volunteers in
these days—people who will allow Him to activate their call
and take risks and do the work of God.

## Define the distinctive of your dream

Passion is a great key to discovering the unique aspect of your
dream. What you are passionate about will usually shape your
call. This is what lights the fire within you. You will campaign
about something that is your passion. You will give money to
and make sacrifices for your passion. It is often the thing that
you enjoy doing and do naturally, not realizing it is your gift
and distinctive. In Romans 12:6–8 we read the wide range of
God's gifts:

> We have different gifts, according to the grace given us. If a
> man's gift is prophesying, let him use it in proportion to his
> faith. If it is serving, let him serve; if it is teaching, let him teach;
> if it is encouraging, let him encourage; if it is contributing to the
> needs of others, let him give generously; if it is leadership, let
> him govern diligently; if it is showing mercy, let him do it
> cheerfully.

We each have different gifts and different levels of grace within
those gifts. Some people are called to teach and are brilliant with
small groups. Other people are called to preach to thousands.

We need to be sure that we operate within our level of grace. So define your passion. Identify what grips your heart. Find out which age and type of people group you love to be with. Discover what you love to do and what is the level of your grace. I have discovered that Gordon, my husband, is one of the best facilitators ever. He loves to work with visionaries and help them birth their dreams. He loves broad strategic administration and giving structure to the visionaries' ideas, but he hates the very detailed paperwork involved. There are others who come to work alongside him who love sorting out his papers and planning the details. Together such people make a fantastic team, and a dream can be born and grow. I have discovered that I love to preach to thousands; in fact, the bigger the better! At first this really concerned me. I thought I must be proud because I enjoyed the large rather than the small, but I have discovered it has to do with gifting. I find I hesitate to speak to a group of fifteen people but would speak to a thousand any day! We have to be real and honest about the gifting God has given us and stop holding it back.

God has given us a wide range of gifts, but they need to work together and function correctly if we are ever to get the job done. The spiritual gifts are not greater than the practical gifts; we need them all. As I have begun to travel more, I have found that my time in the kitchen is limited. So I have been blessed by people in our congregation who have a gift of hospitality. They invite us for special meals, all home-cooked. They bring wonderful baked cakes to our home, and my husband smiles. Their pots of homemade jam are quickly devoured and appreciated. We need these gifts of service.

When I first started ministering in the United Kingdom and I formed my Heartcry team, we had such a mixture of personalities and gifts. One lady, Vron, had a real gift of mercy, and I learned to so appreciate her gift. While I would be preaching with fire and passion and urging people to respond to God, she would notice the hurting and gently hug them and pray with them. She would know instantly who had health problems and who had difficulty walking and spend her time at the conference trying to help their practical needs. She was such a vital part of our team, yet she hated being seen on the platform or being made to pray out loud!

We all have gifts and talents, both natural and spiritual, and we need to allow God to activate them in these days. Ask God to show you how He can use even the areas of your life that seem so natural to you, understanding that there are many people who cannot do the things you find easy. It is time to be abandoned for His purposes!

## Battle for the breakthrough of your destiny

As we begin to acknowledge the true depths of our destiny, we need to realize that it usually takes a lifetime to fulfill our dreams. It takes time for the vision of your heart to be released. Usually there are times when this journey is tough, and it requires us to keep focused and not give up. There is always a battle before we see the word of God over our lives fully birthed, and it is not always easy. Paul encouraged Timothy to persevere and to press into his calling in 2 Timothy 1:6–7:

> For this reason I remind you to fan into flame the gift of God, which is in you through the laying on of my hands. For God did not give us a spirit of timidity, but a spirit of power, of love and of self-discipline.

The gift of God is like a flame burning in the secret place of our being, and we can easily quench it with our fears and feelings of inadequacy. Instead we need to actively fan it into flame with our expectation and faith. Most of us experience overwhelming fears as we begin to take hold of the gift of God imparted to us. So often these fears are not rooted in what other people say to us but what we say to ourselves. We are terrified of being ridiculed and of looking like a fool and failing. The fears that no one will listen to us or help us or that we will lose our friends all paralyze us into inactivity. So here Paul commands Timothy, "Stir up your gift; it is yours. It was given to you by the prophetic word. God dreamed this destiny over your life. Now, Timothy, *do not let fear crush your destiny!*" I believe this is the same message we need to hear: We must conquer our fears and live our destiny!

Many times as we begin to walk into our destiny, we will feel like we are fighting for our lives. It seems that all hell breaks out against us. The battleground can be on every front. You may experience hardship physically and battle with health problems;  you may encounter emotional challenges and find your best friends or leaders betray you; you may feel spiritually that even God has deserted you! My only encouragement is this: It means you are on the right track, not the wrong one! The Bible warns us that as we seek a godly way of life, we will encounter difficulties. We read this in 2 Timothy 3:12: "In fact, everyone who wants to live a godly life in Christ Jesus will be persecuted."

So when you encounter these trials, do not take them as a personal attack, but consider them a badge of honor. You must be doing something right to stir up opposition. The enemy only attacks danger, so you must be invading his territory and causing him trouble. But we also need to recognize that this  battle is not just about our personal breakthrough. It is vital for sowing the seeds that will influence the next generation. It is about that harvest that will flow from *you!* We each need to leave a spiritual inheritance for our children and win the battle of breakthrough for them. I know that each time I stand in faith and minister as a woman, it is a sign to many women that there is a path for them, too. We need heroes who open the way today so that others can walk through the door more easily tomorrow, and then go further.

## Live with yielded obedience

Deep down we know that our life is not our own, but we really need to let this truth sink in deep and examine all the implications. We need to yield everything we have and place it on the altar before God, including our egos and reputation. We need to let this deep cry penetrate heaven: "God, use me. I am Yours, totally surrendered, and I am willing to pay the price!" In Romans 12:1–2, Paul expresses this urgent cry to the Church:

> Therefore, I urge you, brothers, in view of God's mercy, to offer your bodies as living sacrifices, holy and pleasing to God—this is your spiritual act of worship. Do not conform any longer to the pattern of this world, but be transformed by the renewing of your mind. Then you will be able to test and approve what God's will is—his good, pleasing and perfect will.

Sometimes God's ways do not make sense to us from the viewpoint of human logic, but we obey Him anyway. The perfect will of God cannot be analyzed; we just need to get on with it!

When our children were small, I remember there were occasions when I had to go away and preach, leaving Gordon to care for the home and kids. My pride did not like this, and I was worried that people would think I was a poor mother. I was also concerned that my children would grow up hating the ministry and me. I knew that God was asking me to go, but I wanted to stay and look like the perfect mom and wife. So one day God confronted me with this Scripture in Galatians: "Am I now trying to win the approval of men, or of God? Or am I trying to please men? If I were still trying to please men, I would not be a servant of Christ" (1:10).

I felt the challenge of God. I wanted the approval of men; it mattered to me. But I realized that to be obedient I had to die to the approval of men. I have discovered that if you remain gracious, approval usually does come, but only much later! Both of my kids, David and Nicola (now in their twenties), love Jesus, and when we discuss those early days, they admit that there was a cost and they did miss me. But I always remember Nicola saying, "Mom, if God wants you away, we do not want you home because then we will not get blessed!" So pay the price and begin to birth your dream. There will never be a convenient time to obey, so decide to just do it!

## You will never feel that you have enough

However experienced you become and however much you begin to watch your dream become a reality, you will never feel truly confident that you have made it. The battleground may change, but we will always carry the sense of "How can I be doing this?" Remember the little boy who came with his lunch to Jesus in John 6:9? "Here is a boy with five small barley loaves and two small fish, *but how far will they go among so many?*" (emphasis added).

We can feel exactly the same: "How far will what I have go among so much need?" As you begin to step out and live the dream, there will be moments when you feel like the little boy who has only five very ordinary loaves and two very small fish; they look ridiculously small compared to the need. When you look at your resources, you will never have enough. When you keep focused on your ability, you will always feel overwhelmed. Instead, we need to watch the face of Jesus; we need to keep hearing the call of His destiny and His promises over our lives. Then we need to put what we have in our hands into the hands of Jesus and watch how He will multiply it over and over again. If you will yield, you will be amazed to see what God can do with you!

This is the time to acknowledge the fire that is shut up in your bones, to realize that you have a purpose and a destiny, and God wants to use *you* to change *your* world. You have unique gifts and talents, and these are needed in these days to bring change. So do not live a frustrated life of unfulfilled potential, but blow on the flame of your dreams and let the fire burn. In the next chapter we will discover how we walk this journey of discovery and once and for all deal with every dream crusher. Then we will break through to live on the outside the dream we carry on the inside.

# Deal with the Dream Crushers

*"Dreams do not vanish,
so long as people do not abandon them."*
—Phantom F. Harlock

## Kill the dream crushers

As we begin to dare to dream, we must face the challenge of the dream crusher and win. Particularly in European culture, dreamers are often quickly crushed and considered arrogant. As a result, we become fearful of sharing the deep longings of our souls. Unfortunately, we have an environment even in the Church in which people seem to feel it is their job to keep others on the "right track" and be the "voice of reason." This usually means they crush any idea that involves risk and discourage anything new that would take us into uncharted territory. The passion of youthful dreams is quickly quenched with comments like, "Slow down and learn something first," or "I'm the leader; who are you?" or "We've already tried that and it didn't work."

Hope and expectation are easily crushed, but we must reopen the door of hope again and repossess our dreams. We must crush the spirit of the guillotine that just loves to behead any dream before it is born! I have found ministering in the United States so refreshing, as the people are much more receptive toward dreamers. They will encourage your dream, discuss and strategize with you, cheer you on and then help you make your dream happen. However, I have found people are less gracious if you fail and make mistakes; they expect you to succeed. In Europe the people expect everyone to fail!

God wants to restore all those who have had their dreams crushed. Hosea 2:14–15 is a beautiful prophetic picture of this restoration process.

> "Therefore I am now going to allure her;
>    I will lead her into the desert
>    and speak tenderly to her.
> There I will give her back her vineyards,
>    and will make the Valley of Achor [trouble]
>       a door of hope."

For too long we have had this proverb resonating in our minds: "Don't dream too much and you won't be too badly disappointed." But God has spoken over our lives that it is time to live our dreams and not just journal them! So we must walk through the valley of broken dreams and find the keys to the door of hope again. We must allow God to rebuild our trust and value systems, and look for mentors who will shape our dreams with us. There is a voice in the wilderness that will speak to us and bring breakthrough, but we need to see the restoration of our confidence to dream again. We must let the voice of the Great Shepherd allure us and draw us into a place of security and love. As you feel His love touch your life afresh, you will find new hope begin to grow.

If we are going to see creativity grow in our lives again, we need to cultivate an atmosphere of love and trust in the Church. This is the greenhouse of dreams! We need this atmosphere of hope and expectancy to grow in our nation once again so that it shakes loose the hopelessness gripping so many lives. We need to believe that we can win and achieve our dreams and that we will not be humiliated as we try to fulfill our goals.

## Building a greenhouse to grow our dreams again

One of the main reasons the Bible speaks to us so much about the way we talk and about how essential it is to provide a loving, affirming atmosphere is because that is the place that provides space for our dreams to grow. We must learn how to encourage one another into greatness. In fact, that is one of the main purposes of the Church. It should be a place where we go to get encouraged, inspired and built up so that we can build our dreams. The Bible is a book full of great expectations—it encourages us to be what we cannot be naturally and to go where it is impossible to go without God. Jesus said, "What is impossible with men is possible with God" (Luke 18:27).

As we get connected to God, impossible things become possible. However wild and implausible, humanly speaking, your dream from God seems to be, it must be born and live! We must affirm those dreams in one another and learn to encourage and support each other as we push forward. We need to learn to be more willing to trust the fire and passion we see in the eyes of the dreamers. We will never know the end result unless we give people our unqualified permission to have a go.

We must be allowed to grow and explore our dreams and even be allowed to fail before we succeed.

## Identifying the dream crushers

One of the most devastating of all dream crushers is betrayal. If your friend or mentor leaves you and no longer believes in your dream, it crushes the hopes in the deepest place inside you. When your marriage partner no longer wants to live with you and fulfill your dreams of life together, it can feel like the final blow. When betrayal kisses your life, it can feel like you are going to die. But there is a resurrection time for every dream if you will let it grow again. Betrayal is a season we all have to endure, and we must learn to win in this season.

But still the greatest dream crusher is actually ourselves—we are the best at killing our own dreams. So often we blame others for extinguishing our dreams or for causing us frustration in the process of their being born, but more often than not we are the ones who limit our dreams the most. Our fears and hesitations confine our dreams to our minds instead of our lives. We are cautious about sharing the true longings of our hearts in case we are misunderstood or perceived as arrogant. We can feel the fire in our bones, yet we quench this fire with our excuses. We must evaluate the prophetic words over our life and hold them tightly; we must not just dismiss them. We need to heed the words of exhortation given by Paul in 1 Thessalonians 5:19–21: "Do not put out the Spirit's fire; do not treat prophecies with contempt. Test everything. Hold on to the good."

We must hold on to our dreams and let the word of God be birthed through us. We must understand that there is a journey that every dream—and every dreamer—needs to travel before it is born.

## Joseph the dreamer

The most famous dreamer in the Bible has to be Joseph. For the remainder of this chapter I want to look at his life and see how this dreamer became a man who lived his dreams. The challenge, of course, is for us to do the same. As we begin to walk out our dreams, we will recognize the same milestones along the way as on the journey Joseph took. The sequence may differ slightly, but essentially each of us will be confronted by the same issues as Joseph before we can touch and handle the reality of our vision being birthed.

The story of Joseph's life is told in Genesis, from chapter 37 to the end of the book. As you read his story, you realize that here was a man with a dream shut up in his bones from a very young age. He made many mistakes along the way, but when he died he had fulfilled his dreams, and even in death he was still holding on to a dream. Joseph went through seven clear steps in order to birth his dream.

### *1. Somebody will try to kill the dream*

As Joseph's story begins, we discover a son who is greatly loved by his father, Jacob. In this atmosphere of affirmation, he begins to dream of his future. He has some significant spiritual dreams, even though he is still a young man, and quickly realizes that these dreams signify a life of considerable influence. Unfortunately, he does not yet have the wisdom to handle this revelation, and so he begins to talk to those around him about the details. His brothers are not too impressed by his youthful arrogance and are jealous of the favor he has with his dad, especially after his father honors him by giving him a special coat that is richly ornamented. Between them, they decide to kill this dreamer before he becomes much more of a nuisance. Genesis 37:19–20 tells of the plan they hatch to kill his dreams.

"Here comes that dreamer!" they said to each other. "Come now, let's kill him and throw him into one of these cisterns and say that a ferocious animal devoured him. Then we'll see what comes of his dreams."

You can still hear this same sound today. When you are carrying a God-dream and it begins to be noticed by your friends and family, you will often find that you enter a season of misunderstanding when they will try to kill the dream within you. Or, even worse, you may feel they are just trying to kill *you*! The enemy loves to stir up the sound of mockery to kill your dream: "Oh, here comes that dreamer. She believes that God is going to give them land to build a new pregnancy crisis center in the middle of town!" or "Here comes that dreamer. He's crazy; he believes that he can grow a church of five thousand people in this little town!" The enemy always wants to kill the dream and sometimes the dreamer, too!

I remember when Gordon and I first felt we should go to Africa as missionaries. Even though both of us have parents who are godly and wonderful people, they had real issues about us wanting to leave the United Kingdom. As we shared our vision, they shared their concerns, and it felt like our dream of Africa was being crushed. In the end we waited for one year while we prayed and tried to work out what all this advice meant, until one day we both knew we had to go with or without their blessing. We visited our parents again and told them the news, but this time we began to see them smile. Finally, we were able to leave for Africa with their full blessing, but for one year it felt like our dreams were being crushed.

When a dream is new and fragile, it is often hard to handle the criticism and questions that arise, but this process will strengthen your call. It clarifies your purpose and kills any emotional unrealism. So as you step out, do not be surprised if people pour cold water on your dreams. Do not react negatively when this happens. Instead, hold fast to your vision and press through the fire.

## 2. The context of the dream will often change

When we begin to process our vision, we usually try to interpret its meaning in the context of our current circumstances. When Joseph dreamed, his dream used the language of his present-day life. The language was agriculture and family. There was no mention of Egypt! I expect he thought initially that somehow this dream would involve his family in the fields at home. Maybe he thought it was a promise that at some time all the family would gather around him, there would be reconciliation and he would be loved by his brothers. We do not know what he thought the dreams meant. But we do know that he was not expecting to go to Egypt.

This is the same for many of us. Most of us think we have understood the implications and application of the vision we are carrying, but then we find we have to adjust these thoughts throughout our lives. We usually do not understand the full context of our dreams until later. I remember learning this lesson a few years ago. I was ministering in Birmingham one Saturday when I gave a prophetic word to a woman. I said to her, "God says that the dream you have held for the last seventeen years is ready to be birthed. You have been through a time of great trial, but in six weeks you will begin to see a change, and then your dream will begin to be birthed." The woman cried as I gave her the word, and then I did not see her again for over three years. When I did meet her again, she said, "Rachel, I need to talk to you!" and she told me this story:

> When you gave me that word, I had been dreaming of running a center for young teenage boys who were without any real home life. I have always wanted to help young lads find a family. So

when you said, "Your dream of seventeen years is going to be birthed in the next six weeks," I was so excited! You see, I was saved seventeen years ago, and my husband is still not saved. I have always imagined that my husband will get saved, and we will go to Romania or Africa or somewhere like that and have a children's home for young men, and then I would be satisfied! So I thought that your word meant that in six weeks my husband would be saved, and then we would move as missionaries to another nation. Well, here is what actually happened: Six weeks after you prayed for me, my husband left me, leaving the divorce papers on the table one morning. I was devastated. What would happen to my dreams now? But I kept thinking of the six weeks, and so I prayed. I have three sons, and so I had to tell them that their daddy had left.

As we sat and cried, I was so angry and thought my dreams were finished and that you had lied! But a few months later the school contacted me and asked me if I would be willing to come and speak to some classes of teenagers about handling life when the father leaves home. Apparently the staff had noticed that my sons were handling the home situation so well that they wanted me to come and share the wisdom I had used with them. At first I was very nervous, but I went.

God blessed these classes and more opportunities opened up. Now the local council has approached me and given me the use of a community center in the area. I now have helpers, and we have a center for teenage children who need counseling and help because they have been through tough times at home. I am now doing what I had always dreamed about, but I *never* thought it would happen like this. A couple of years ago I thought I was dying, but now I am living life to the full. <u>My dream has come true, just in a very different way!</u>

### 3. We receive the dream and then the training

Usually we have the revelation of what God has in store for us before we receive the training or have the character to do the job. Having been sold into captivity in Egypt, Joseph finds himself placed into the house of a man called Potiphar, where he begins to learn about administration in an Egyptian household. At this time he does not realize that he is going to organize the entire Egyptian nation during a time of national crisis. Here God is positioning him, without him even understanding what is happening, in the perfect position to get the training he needs. We read that Joseph did well and learned how to run all the affairs of this home.

> From the time he put him in charge of his household and of all that he owned, the LORD blessed the household of the Egyptian because of Joseph. The blessing of the LORD was on everything Potiphar had, both in the house and in the field. So he left in Joseph's care everything he had; with Joseph in charge, he did not concern himself with anything except the food he ate.
>
> Genesis 39:5–6

Often we do not understand some of the job changes we encounter, the training courses that we get sent on or the languages we are asked to learn, because at the time they do not seem relevant. But later, when we look back, we can see how all these tiny threads of our life are woven together to make the tapestry of our calling complete. We need to be trained, and so we may need to move location and travel to different places before we can develop the gifts we need to fulfill our dreams.

I remember that when Gordon and I were first married, God called him to leave his job and start his own company. This was a tough season in our lives as we pioneered this new company. The financial pressure was huge, but again and again we learned lessons of faith and found God was able to provide. Many of the lessons of faith that we would need later while on the mission field, we learned in the boardroom while in business. Without us even being aware, God had been training us for the ministry.

As you look at your job and your nine-to-five existence, you may feel that it is so irrelevant to the calling that you carry, but I would just encourage you, do not despise the day of small beginnings. You never know what doors these little keys may open. As you are faithful in the little matters, you will find that God has a plan, and you are being trained for your future.

### 4. You will be betrayed

Most of us would love to skip this stage of the preparation. None of us likes the thought of being betrayed. However, I believe that it is a vital step in the process and one that every leader will encounter at least once in his or her life. As we read the Bible, we can immediately see the pattern: David was betrayed by his wife Michal who mocked him, by his son Absalom, by his officials and by others; Jesus was betrayed by Judas, Peter and others; and of course Joseph was betrayed by his brothers.

Just when Joseph is doing well and life is looking great, suddenly he finds himself in an uncomfortable situation with Potiphar's wife. She tries to seduce him repeatedly, but he rightly refuses. However, Potiphar's wife feels insulted by his constant refusals, and one day she accuses him of rape. So Joseph is sent to prison unjustly.

> Then she told [Potiphar] this story: "That Hebrew slave you brought us came to me to make sport of me. But as soon as I screamed for help, he left his cloak beside me and ran out of the house." When his master heard the story his wife told him, saying, "This is how your slave treated me," he burned with anger. Joseph's master took him and put him in prison.
>
> verses 17–20

Like Joseph, so often the betrayal we experience touches our very integrity. Joseph was accused of rape when in fact he had done everything he could to keep himself morally pure! He was totally innocent, yet his trust was abused and he was betrayed. I have found this to be true in my life. It is in the very area where you believe you are doing right and keeping the right attitude that you find you are accused and betrayed. I remember soon after I started ministering in Norway, I was accused of fabricating the story about my healing after my road accident. I have always tried to keep my integrity in the place of ministry and tell the absolute truth without embellishing it, and here I was being accused of lying about one of the toughest seasons of my life. I even had the evidence to prove it was true, but no one wanted to listen, so I was persecuted on a website for a couple of years and had to hold my peace.

During this season I discovered that betrayal exposes your heart like no other situation. You feel raw and vulnerable, and the real you is revealed! As I learned to accept this season of persecution and did not try to defend myself, I found that a fresh grace began to fill me, and a new confidence that God was my shield and defender began to grow. I could do nothing to stop the betrayal of my trust, but I realized God knew the truth and that was all that mattered. Even when Joseph was finally released from jail, we never read that all the charges were dropped and his name was cleared. He probably lived with the taint of that accusation against him all his life, but he and God knew the truth, so he was free!

## 5. You will enter a season of confinement

Just when you feel that things could not get any better, suddenly everything goes wrong, and you are sent to "jail." It is like playing a children's board game where you have nearly won the jackpot but with just one throw of the dice, you are suddenly back near the start all over again! Just when you feel you can smell the breakthrough and everything is going the right way, you suddenly discover that a vital person on your team has decided to leave. Just when you can see the break-through season coming, you lose your job and you have to move. You feel like you have been sent to prison and you begin to wonder, *How can my dream happen now?*

This is what happened to Joseph, but his attitude, even in this place of constraint, always challenges me. We read the following:

> But while Joseph was there in the prison, the LORD was with him; he showed him kindness and granted him favor in the eyes of the prison warden. So the warden put Joseph in charge of all those held in the prison, and he was made responsible for all that was done there. The warden paid no attention to anything under Joseph's care, because the LORD was with Joseph and gave him success in whatever he did.
>
> verses 20–23

Even though Joseph was in a completely different set of external circumstances, his internal attitude and his work ethic did not change. He was still faithful and worked well, keeping everything in perfect order. He was under the favor of God even though he appeared to be in a place of judgment. But because he kept a right attitude, he still flourished even in the place of constraint.

Like Joseph, you will experience sudden limitations that come upon your life and seem to prevent the breakthrough of your dreams. You suddenly discover you are pregnant, and with more children on the way, everything has to go on hold. You find that just as you are about to step out and live your dream, your financial situation changes drastically, and you have to go to work again. Or you are just about to pioneer a new venture with a group of people when one of the key players moves away. Perhaps you discover that just when you think you are free to pursue your dream, your time is totally limited because an elderly parent comes to live with you. All these situations can make us feel like our dreams have been sent to jail, but do not fear; there is a perfect time for everything, and it will come. The challenge from the life of Joseph is this: How will we serve when the dreams of our hearts seem to move further away?

### 6. You will serve someone else's dream before you have your own

This season in jail can last a long time, and Joseph must have despaired at times. But then the cupbearer and the baker, men imprisoned with him, enter Joseph's life. One night they both begin to dream. In the morning they look dejected, and when Joseph asks them what is wrong, they reply that they have no one to interpret their dreams. So Joseph listens to their dreams and tells them that in three days Pharaoh will restore the cupbearer to his previous position, but the baker will be killed. He gives them accurate interpretations that prove to be true. He then asks the cupbearer to remember him when his time of release comes. We read, "But when all goes well with you, remember me and show me kindness; mention me to Pharaoh and get me out of this prison" (40:14).

However, even though Joseph appeals to the cupbearer to help him, and he has served him by interpreting his dream correctly, the cupbearer does not help Joseph: "The chief cupbearer, however, did not remember Joseph; he forgot him" (verse 23).

I always find it incredible that even after all Joseph's help, the cupbearer did not help Joseph. This can be true for us, too. Maybe you have been waiting for a long time, burning with a passion for the nations. You have sat in your church with this vision for years when two new people walk into the congregation. The pastor turns to you and asks you to help them get their vision for missions established in the church. At first you are speechless; you've waited years to be able to birth your heart for missions in the church, but now you are being asked to help someone else with their dream, and yours is forgotten! When you are asked to facilitate someone else's dream like this, how will you serve? Here Joseph served well and then had to wait another two years before anyone noticed him again!

This is always a tough time, but if you do not pass this test and allow bitterness to grow, it will crush your dream. If you react badly in these circumstances, your thoughts will become such a distraction that your dream will get polluted and the dream crusher will win. We must learn to win in this season of serving others, especially when we feel overlooked and forgotten.

### 7. Your dream will come true—and suddenly

Joseph waits another two years, and then Pharaoh begins to dream! Now Joseph is called out of the prison and summoned to the palace, where he is asked to interpret the dreams. Suddenly Joseph is standing on the threshold of his destiny as he realizes that this dream involves him:

> Then Pharaoh said to Joseph, "Since God has made all this known to you, there is no one so discerning and wise as you. You shall be in charge of my palace, and all my people are to submit to your orders. Only with respect to the throne will I be greater than you."
>
> 41:39–40

Finally Joseph had broken through, and his dreams were in his hand. One minute there was no change, and the next minute it was all change. Now the dream crusher was defeated and Joseph was standing in his dream at last.

It is the same with our lives. We can struggle and feel so overwhelmed, but then suddenly one action can start a landslide and everything changes. I have learned that however much you plan and expect your dream to come true, it always happens suddenly! Just like writing this book. I had dreamed about writing a book for many years; I had many prophecies about writing given to me, but I did not know where to start. Then one day I received an email from Tim Pettingale at New Wine Press, and the rest is history. The book that I dreamed about has been written and published!

There are many opportunities for the dream crushers to kill our dreams along the way, but we need to win this battle. Joseph kept his heart right throughout his journey, and when he did finally connect with his brothers again, he could see beyond their actions to the purposes of God.

> "And now, do not be distressed and do not be angry with yourselves for selling me here, because it was to save lives that God sent me ahead of you. For two years now there has been famine in the land, and for the next five years there will not be plowing and reaping. But God sent me ahead of you to preserve for you a remnant on earth and to save your lives by a great deliverance."
>
> 45:5–7

There have been many times in my life that I have been just about to give up when I sensed that I must stand firm and see what happens. Get ready for your sudden breakthrough, because you *will* conquer your dream crushers. Here is an email I received from a young couple who tried for a long time to conceive. I hope it will inspire you to hold on to your dreams and see the breakthrough.

Well, God has done it! We have had a true miracle—Kate is nearly thirteen weeks pregnant! After nearly a year of seeing a specialist and undergoing lots of tests, they told us that basically it wasn't going to happen and told us to think about the possibility of adoption. Well, that was December, and I must admit it hit me pretty hard, but I have to say Kate never started doubting and believed God would overcome that (I tell you, her faith is incredible). Anyway, a few weeks later Kate was pregnant! Thank you for the really spot-on words given to us that helped us hope and dream. God has been amazing! We know it is due to some very faithful friends who have prayed for us, and we want to thank you so much for your prayers. I am still overwhelmed by it but very excited.

Pete and Kate

# CHAPTER 6

# Dreamers Who Birth Their Dreams

*"Some men see things as they are*
*and say, 'Why?'*
*I dream of things that never were*
*and say, 'Why not?'"*
—George Bernard Shaw

Once we know we are carrying the dream of God in our being, what are we going to do? Like Jeremiah, we begin to say and feel, "Your word [dream] is like a fire in my bones, and I am weary of holding it in!" (see Jeremiah 20:9). There comes a time when we can no longer carry the dream inside us; we have to birth the dream. John 1:14 speaks of Jesus as being the Word but then states this Word became flesh and dwelled among us. There is a time when the word of God has to be fleshed out and become a reality, not just a dream. What does this birthing process look like? We have to move from words to action; we have to take hold of the dream spiritually and then practically. We first birth the dream by prayer spiritually, and then we have to *do something*!

## Royal intercession

I believe there is a desperate sound of intercession that needs to awaken in the Church. This is not the sound of nice, polite prayer but the tearing sound of prayer that births the dreams of God. Many of us have carried the word of God in our spirits for too long, and now it is time to be the generation of dreamers who birth their dreams through faith and hard work. This labor of love first has to start on our knees as we take hold of the word of God and pray!

Most of us are too familiar with the Scripture in 1 Peter 2:9 that says, "You are a chosen people, a royal priesthood, a holy nation, a people belonging to God, that you may declare the praises of him who called you out of darkness into his wonderful light."

For a long time I have understood the fact that we function as priests in our role of prayer, but only recently I realized we are called to be a "royal" priesthood, not just priests. I began to wonder, what distinctive does a *royal* priesthood have? A priest is someone who stands before God pleading for the sake of the people, so what would *royal intercession* sound like? As I began to study the Bible, I began to notice the theme of our royal lineage, and then God drew my attention to some verses in Psalm 45, where we read:

> All glorious is the princess within [her chamber];
> > her gown is interwoven with gold.
> In embroidered garments she is led to the king;
> > her virgin companions follow her
> > and are brought to you.
> They are led in with joy and gladness;
> > they enter the palace of the king.
>
> Your sons will take the place of your fathers;
> > *you will make them princes throughout the land.*
>
> verses 13–16, emphasis added

God began to speak to me that we, this present generation of believers, are to "make ... princes throughout the land." In other words, we must raise up and disciple the next generation to carry their royal heritage as children of the King. It struck me that the verse says "you [i.e., you and me] will make them princes." It is not something God will do for us, but something for which we must take responsibility. How can we do this? This awareness of our royal destiny flows out of the place of intimacy with our Father. It comes when we, the Bride of Christ, have been in the chamber of the King. When we have been in the presence of God, there is a sense of His royalty conferred upon us that releases a new flow of dignity and authority that will affect us and those who come into contact with us. We need to pass this on to the next generation and see them flourish as princes and priests in the land.

The final verse of Psalm 45 says, "I will perpetuate your memory through all generations; therefore the nations will praise you for ever and ever" (verse 17). When we have the right understanding of our position as children of the King of Kings, people will look at us and sense there is something different and will be drawn to the One to whom we are related. When people look at our lives, they should discern a "royal connection," a divine authority that distinguishes us from other people.

Proverbs 31 carries the same kind of thought as it talks about the wife of great virtue: "Her children arise and call her blessed; her husband also, and he praises her" (verse 28). In the same way, as we receive the revelation that we are part of the ultimate "royal family," our behavior and bearing will impact everyone around us. When you are walking in the light of this revelation, other areas of life will come into alignment: Your marriage will be blessed; your children will grow up with right attitudes.

## A new authority to birth our dreams

God wants to give us a whole new understanding of the *impartation* we receive in our lives in that place of intimacy. Once we have been wooed into the bridal chamber and have spent time alone with Jesus, the King of Kings, something special happens. The word of God comes to us, the Holy Spirit overshadows us and, like Mary, we find that a destiny seed is planted in our spirits. We now carry the dream of God, but we still need to birth this dream. A new authority comes upon us, and the more time we spend with our King Jesus, the more this authority increases. Suddenly, a godly authority is in our DNA; it becomes a part of who we are. We know we are not carrying out our ideas and instructions anymore, but we are messengers carrying the word of God, and it is His dream being carried in our life! We have a royal bearing, and we know it. This is not arrogance; it is simply confidence in our relationship. When you are adopted into a royal family, what do you become? What is your title? You are a prince or a princess! But in our heavenly family it is even more than that—we become a prince of princes or a princess of princesses, because He is the King of Kings!

Prophetically there is a new sound of authority and declaration that God wants to release through His Church in this hour. It is the day for declarative prayer, the day for royal intercession, the day to issue a royal decree over our nations that things *will* change! We can speak with confidence because we know we have the ear of the mighty King of Kings and we know His desires. A new cry will ring out across our nations that will begin to enforce the written judgments of God. Psalm 149 says our responsibility will be "to carry out the sentence written against them. This is the glory of all his saints" (verse 9).

We have a royal mandate, a royal decree, that we must begin

to declare to the nations. It is time for the Church to speak out, saying, "It is written; take notice. The will of God is being accomplished." We do not come as priests, pleading for God to fulfill His word, but as the children of the Most High God, knowing that God has already determined and decided what we now declare.

If we are to be effective, however, it is critical that we have regular times of real intimacy with the King. Spiritual authority is imparted to us after we have been in the King's presence. Once we know we have heard what He has said, we can then repeat what we have heard, knowing that we speak the King's words. Nothing will happen if we bypass this audience with the King and simply declare what we think should be prayed. Now is not the time to birth our good ideas, but to carry and declare the dream of God over our communities and nations.

The dreams we will carry for our communities and nations are not going to be the usual ideas carried by average people. We will dream big and will need to take risks of faith. Our dreams will be too big for our bank account and too unrealistic for our abilities, but God will trigger these unreasonable desires in our hearts. For such dreams to be born, we need to know whom we belong to and what He has said. Out of that connection will come a strategy that is genuine. Some people make an empty declaration lacking any faith and conviction because they have learned the vision and language from somebody else. There is no substance to it because it is not a dream imparted by God; it is just a good idea they have heard. Our words only have substance when we have been with the King and know that He has impregnated us with His passion and word for our world.

Recently when I was asked to suggest a theme for a women's conference, I gave the title "You Are a Princess." I was surprised when the conference organizers squirmed and wanted to use a different title. They were concerned and gave excuses like, "It sounds too presumptuous"; "It's too arrogant"; and "Women don't want to be princesses." Immediately, their reaction told me something: It is clear that the Church has lost the sense of our royal heritage!

All of us have seen the effects of poor and hesitating leadership in our nations, our workplaces, our schools, even our families. I believe we must raise up leaders in the land who have a real sense of godly authority and direction. We need to put the dignity back into our society. Most people believe that they are worthless and their lives will never achieve much, but God has placed His DNA in our blood, and He wants us to be history makers and city shakers. He has put a dream of change within us and wants us to stand, speak and make a difference.

When Princess Diana was pregnant, everyone knew that it was *impossible* for her to give birth to a nobody. Everyone knew she would give birth to a crown prince because she herself was a princess. In the same way, we need to understand that we are not raising up a generation of nobodies! It is *impossible* for the King of Kings to give birth to a nobody. It is insulting to suggest that you are a nobody if you are connected to the King of Kings! It goes against His very nature. You are a prince or princess connected to the Kingdom of God. We need to walk out the mandate conceived by His Spirit on the inside of us, without apology.

We need to protect and mentor the dreams of the next generation and help those people be released into godly, governmental roles. We need to position ourselves so that power will flow down from the Godhead through us and help release a new generation of leaders and entrepreneurs to live their dreams and push forward the boundaries of the Kingdom of God. History teaches us that the Church has always been at the forefront of community transformation. The Church was instrumental in founding most of the great institutions of society. The Church has helped fashion democratic government, politics, law; the Church has built hospitals and schools all over the world and has been a strong influence in our health and educational programs. The Church has always produced leaders who were instrumental in societal change. It is time for such princes and princesses to arise in the land again.

In the United Kingdom, we are more accustomed to the protocols of royalty and the aristocracy since we have our royal family and not a president. We understand that certain people receive a title like *lord* or *lady* at birth simply because they inherit this title from their family. However, other people in the United Kingdom can also have titles bestowed on them in recognition of the way in which they have served their nation. There is a difference between these two groups of people that is interesting. Those who earn a title through service never quite seem to carry their title with as much ease as those who were born with a title. It is just not in their DNA, and they have not been raised with the training and the expectation of the title. Most of those who are born into a family with a title are fairly indifferent about the fact, and they do not keep reminding others that they have a title. They just are who they are.

As we begin to realize the authority that is part of our godly heritage, we do not strut about parading it arrogantly, but with grace and humility we walk with an assurance and a confidence, knowing that we are backed by all the royal authority of heaven. People with a royal heritage have connections. They know people in high places! You know that if they offer to speak on your behalf, they will be able to do something for you.

## A royal decree

First Peter 2:9 says that we are a chosen people. Note that it does not say "one day you will be," but "you are"! And the purpose is this: "that you may *declare* the praises of him who called you out of darkness into his wonderful light" (emphasis added).

To *declare* is a word with royal connotations. This declaration is a royal decree. The Greek word used here most often refers to the angels who come from the presence of God with good news to celebrate and declare to the world. This suggests that we should declare with absolute confidence what the King has expressed should happen. But too often we struggle with the concept that we are a chosen people with a royal mandate. Often we come to God in desperation, and our tone is pleading. We sound like we are the servant begging our master to listen to us. We approach God a bit like the prodigal son: "O Lord, I'm not worthy." But our prayers should not consist of, "God, help me, help me!" Instead, God wants us to pray with a royal bearing, with a dignity and strength that reveals our royal heritage. When you know you are a prince or princess, your prayers have a completely different tone and sound to them.

If you grew up as a member of the royal family in the United Kingdom, then you would consider Buckingham Palace to be your "normal" house, and all the land behind it would be your normal backyard. When the royal children were small, they probably thought every kid had a garden that size! In the same way, God wants us to pray with that kind of understanding of His Kingdom. He is the King of Kings, and we are princes and princesses in His Kingdom. His backyard is our backyard! The world is our turf because it belongs to God. We do not need to plead to have access to it. It has already been given to us; it is our birthright as children of the Kingdom.

As children of God, thinking big should be normal for us because we are connected to the God who created the universe! It is in our spiritual DNA. As we pray, *big* should not be a problem. We must encourage those who dream big dreams for

God to continue to do so, because with God everything is possible. One of the enemies of the dreamers in the Church is the atmosphere created by dream crushers. This atmosphere of unbelief and cynicism, hopelessness and apathy, tries to abort the dreams of God that we have been ordained to carry. Before we can even bring our dreams to birth, the dragon is at the mouth of our womb and tries to destroy our dreams. But God spoke to me a little while ago and said, *Do not fear. I designed your spirits to be My dream catchers. Catch My dreams for your generation, hide them in your heart and pray, and you will bring to birth healthy "babies" fully formed. The enemy will not be able to abort your dreams if you support and encourage each other and dream together of My Kingdom.* The enemy sets out to crush our dreams before they can come to fruition, but we need to have a new cry and declare, "Let Your Kingdom come and Your will be done on this earth!"

## Princes and princesses in places of influence

As we watch the nations, I see a new breed of "ordinary people" carrying this royal DNA who are ready to arise and impact our cities. They will become a generation of reformers and entrepreneurs and those who gain their breakthrough and birth their dreams. For too long the Church has neglected her responsibility to get involved in big projects of change.

I want to tell you the story of a girl called Rosemary, who at one time belonged to my mentoring group before moving to the United States. Rosemary originally came from Ghana to live in England with her family, who were first-generation British. Right from her younger years, Rosemary wanted God to use her in the political arena for change. A woman of prayer, Rosemary kept asking God to use her and found that God fast-tracked her into His purposes. She went to college and became involved in politics. In a very short time she was invited to become the international liaison officer for the Labour Party. She was offered the opportunity to shadow the foreign and defense ministers as they conducted their business. Later she was asked to write briefing papers and speech outlines concerning the government's policies in the Middle East.

I asked Rosemary how she handled this influential work. She said to me, "I watch all the politics. I watch what is going on, and as I sit at my desk typing these speeches, I pray, 'O God, let Your Kingdom come, let Your will be done.'" As she is working, she is speaking the royal decrees of the Lord over the nations and situations He has allowed her to be involved in. Rosemary has had the opportunity to preside over foreign policy briefings that have been read out by the government in places of influence, having soaked the speech with the purposes of God in prayer.

After a while Rosemary asked us to pray for her, that she would have an opportunity to get involved in the United Nations. She felt that this was the next step in God's plan for her. She made a decision to move sideways in her political career in order to take a three-month job in New York so she could be based close to the UN offices. Her plan was to literally position herself nearby so that she could accept the right job if it came up. All her colleagues thought she was taking a huge risk to make such a move, but we had prayed about it and had received a real peace from God that it was the right thing to do. A job came up before her temporary job finished, she was interviewed and she got the job!

Rosemary is still young, but she is now based in New York, working in the UN building and working directly with the UN development program. Now her papers have been read on the floor of the United Nations, and she is involved in influencing how the United Nations serves other nations. She dreamed that she would be used to sound the heartcry of justice, to be a part of breaking the spirit of poverty in the world. This royal intercessor is sitting where God intended her to be, speaking out His words over the nations.

## Privilege and responsibility

There are belief systems we have in the Church that I believe God wants to radically change once and for all. Both as individuals and as the corporate Church, we need to deal with the language of rejection that so influences our outlook on life and totally contradicts God's language of royalty and dignity. Did you know that you are related to the most famous person who has ever walked the earth? The Bible says that Jesus is your brother! Jesus Christ is the most famous person in the history of the world. His Book has outsold every other book in history. What a privileged position we are in. But with privilege comes responsibility.

If we knew that whatever we said or did would have serious and far-reaching implications for a famous family member, we would learn to be very careful about how we lived our life. We would realize that wherever we went, people would know our face and our name, too—and if we spoke out of turn or said something we should not, it would be all over the front pages of the newspapers. We are all familiar with the bad press given to the royal family's children when they misbehave! We have that same level of responsibility as "heirs of the Father"— brothers and sisters of Jesus. It means we have to conduct ourselves rightly. The Church needs to clean up her act. The fact that many members of the Church have behaved badly in public is the reason why so many people are offended or turned off by the Church. They see the Church as a place for hypocrites who do not live up to the standards of their famous relative.

Playtime is over now. It is time to grow up and be princes and princesses in the land.

## A season of partnership

In order to take our place as children of the King and birth our dreams, we need to realize that we cannot do it alone in isolation. We are in a season of partnership. We will not be able to birth our dreams alone because our God-given dreams are intended for the benefit of His Kingdom, not merely for us personally. God requires that we work with others in order to see His purposes fulfilled. As it is in the natural, so it is in the spiritual. We will find that there are people who are like mothers carrying the burden of the dream as if pregnant, and others who come alongside like good midwives, helping to birth the dream so that it does not die in the process! We need to seek those Kingdom connections that will help us incubate and then birth the dream.

Most of us now realize that one church will not bring revival to a city, but together, with an attitude of unity, we will change the atmosphere. God has been challenging our independence and stirring an attitude of partnership. We see these partnerships working at many levels of church and society. If we are going to see a nation change, then we must recognize these God-connections.

Some of the partnerships I see coming together to birth these dreams are:

1. Partnership of genders: God is increasingly bringing men and women to work together for His Kingdom purpose, supporting one another and recognizing the gifting of each gender. Rather than living with a fearful or dominating attitude toward each other, we are learning to work together and get the job done.

2.  Partnership of generations: God is the God of three generations working together—Abraham, Isaac and Jacob. If we are going to birth the dreams of God, then we must also cooperate with the generational plan of God.

3.  Partnership of nations: God is the Creator of the nations, and the Holy Spirit is an international Spirit. We know that in the last days, every tribe, tongue and nation will bow together, and so we must see God's bigger plan for the nations. In our cities and communities today, we find the nations are widely represented, so as dreamers we need to dream together and let the DNA of the nations be birthed.

4.  Partnership of denominations: It is time for us to realize that we need varied expressions of church to come together to reach a city. We need to learn to respect each other and our mutual love for Jesus and His word. Though we may have different expressions, language and priorities of service, we do have the same Jesus! We need to know that no church can save the people; only Jesus can, as only Jesus died for them. Our task is to gather around His name and lift Him up. As these different expressions come together in unity, there will be a greater influence from the churches in our communities.

5.  Partnership of church leadership and marketplace leaders: For too long church leaders have given the impression that they see business leadership and marketplace positions as second-class positions in the Kingdom of God. But today we are realizing that God has placed many men and women in the community in positions of influence to be a voice that helps the church bring change. I believe that this connection between church leaders and business and political leaders is essential if we are ever going to see our dreams birthed in our cities. We need the expertise and

influence of marketplace leaders to help us accelerate the birthing of our dreams.

6. Partnership of vision and provision: We need to realize that if we are going to birth our dreams, we must see a significant release of finances for the Kingdom of God. Some people are called to be visionaries, and they carry the vision of the dream, but other people are called to be the support team, to come alongside the vision and to help birth it with their practical expertise.

## The vision and provision working together

I believe that in these days this strong partnership between the people of vision and provision is essential if we are ever going to get the job done. We see this partnership working together in Luke chapter 5. Here we read:

> When he had finished speaking, he said to Simon, *"Put out into deep water, and let down the nets for a catch."*
> Simon answered, "Master, we've worked hard all night and haven't caught anything. But because you say so, I will let down the nets."
> When they had done so, they caught such a large number of fish that their nets began to break. *So they signaled their partners in the other boat to come and help them,* and they came and filled both boats so full that they began to sink.
>
> verses 4–7, emphasis added

Here we see Jesus calling to Peter, challenging him to step out into a new place: "Put out into deep water." This is the call that every visionary hears; it disturbs you and triggers the process of change. God challenges us to step out into our dreams. Often, like Peter, we find that once we step out, we realize we are in deep water and in danger of sinking! When you feel that the dream and the vision of God is too big and you feel over-whelmed, that is the time you need to signal to your partners and ask them to come and help you. Here we read that Peter called his partners for assistance. Too often dreams and projects fail because we do not have a relationship with a boat of provision that can come and work alongside our vision. We step out into deep water alone and independent, and when we begin to feel like we are sinking, we have no friends in another boat who can come and help. This is a day of relationships, and we need to have the boat of vision working alongside the boat of provision if we are going to see the dream birthed success-fully. Here this partnership was successful, and we read that *both* boats were filled! They fulfilled the vision and returned satisfied and full, whether they were the boat of vision or provision.

## A season of preparation

During this season of waiting and birthing, the true identity of the Church is being prepared. Although we may have many dreams of the Kingdom work to which we have been called, God has a dream for the King. The most significant dream that must be birthed is the dream of God to have a Bride for His heavenly Bridegroom! We are those being prepared for this purpose. We are being prepared for a royal wedding. We need to be ready to be extravagant lovers of God, called to a much deeper level of intimacy than most of us have yet experienced. We need to get ready to be with the King of Kings in His bridal chamber.

Throughout the Church there has been such emotional poverty. People do not really believe that God has made them valuable and significant. In fact, many of us are irritated by those who seem to be secure in their destiny and dreams. We often consider them arrogant or overconfident. But God wants us to be free from all the rubble that has blocked our dreaming capacity and closed our emotions. He wants to heal all the woundedness that causes us to believe we are not valuable and not able to do what He has said.

In Genesis 26:15 we read how Isaac discovered that all the wells that had been dug by his father and his father's servants had been stopped up with earth by their Philistine enemies. I believe our Father has given us many generational dreams and visions, and the devil has been busy filling up those wells and trying to stem the flow of this revelation. But it is time to let heaven open these wells of revelation again, so that in seeking Him we might find a fresh revelation of who we are and what we are called to do in these days.

We need to unblock what the enemy has blocked. Wherever I go in the world, I find the enemy has the same strategy: to rob the Church of her destiny and dignity. I can give an altar call for those who suffer from rejection, insecurity, inferiority, lack of value, lack of significance—and the vast majority will respond. Fear and rejection, these twin enemies, have come against the Church and society like a virulent plague and gripped many lives. Why? Because this atmosphere will destroy our ability to dream and prevent us from trusting God and fulfilling His purposes in our lives. If these two things are gripping you, you can never really know that you are loved and accepted.

We are never going to be a royal priesthood that can confidently take our place of authority until these things in our lives are dealt with. Today is the day when God wants to give you a revelation of His love for you and show you how valuable and significant you are. You can stand tall with your head up and shoulders back, look people in the eye and say, "I'm a prince of God!" or "I'm a princess of God!" God is love, and God loves all He has made. The greatest perversion and lie of the devil, therefore, is rejection. Rejection is a deception, because God never rejects us! It is absolutely contrary to God's very nature.

God had to work this revelation deep into my life so that I could be and do what He made me to. Today people know me as an outgoing, confident person, but I was not always the way I am now. At the age of seventeen, I was withdrawn and insecure. If I entered a room full of people on any social occasion, I would dive for the chair in the corner, where I could hide. My greatest nightmare was to stand up and speak in public. I hated giving people eye contact when I was speaking to them. In fact, the first time Gordon told me that he loved me, I wanted to run and hide! The first time he tried to kiss me, I pushed him away. *Nobody can love me like that*, I thought. *I'm not valuable*. How could this be when I had a Christian upbringing with godly parents who loved me? It proves that it really does not matter what your background is; the same wretched devil tries to convince each of us that we are nothing, going nowhere, doing irrelevant things.

Sometimes when I am asked to speak in front of thousands of people, I want to laugh, because I think, *Wow, God has been so good to me; He has delivered me from all my fears! Who would imagine that the old Rachel would be doing this?* But one day the old Rachel had a revelation: I realized I was living gripped by strong deception, and it controlled my life. I was hiding in my "poor little me" world and was busy being a victim when suddenly God showed me that my rejection was an evil deception from the enemy, and I had better learn to hate it. I realized this mindset was absolutely contrary to the character of God. God is love. Every time we say, "I'm worthless, I'm useless, I'm not valuable," we are pushing God away. It is like saying to God, "I don't believe you. You're a liar!"

Would you rather believe your feelings? Would you rather believe yourself or God? God has poured out His love upon us in an extraordinarily extravagant way. We had better believe it and resist all deception that challenges God's character! We have to shake off every bit of rejection. We need to replace the word *rejection* with *deception*. Do you want to live in deception? I know I do not! Break that lie and live in what God has declared over you. You are not a failure; you are not too fat, too thin, too clever or not clever enough. You are a well-loved and much-desired royal child who belongs to an incredible family!

Matthew 22:37–39 says,

> Jesus replied: " 'Love the Lord your God with all your heart and with all your soul and with all your mind.' This is the first and greatest commandment. And the second is like it: 'Love your neighbor as yourself.' "

I want to emphasize this last phrase of Jesus: "Love your neighbor as yourself." The implication is that we *should* love ourselves. We will have a serious problem loving our neighbors correctly if we cannot even love ourselves. This, I believe, is one of the core reasons that so much of the Church has a problem with evangelism. The Bible says that it is the revelation of this love of God that "compels" us. So if we do not really love ourselves correctly because we do not live in the revelation of His love, then we will be lacking this essential motivation. We need to be internally motivated by the love of God into the harvest fields of our community.

We need to be healed in order to love correctly, and then we will be confident to risk again and step out. We have to be able to truly love God with all our being and have our self-image transformed. Then we can extend God's love to others in a dynamic and powerful way. In order to reach the broken-hearted of our communities, we need a deeper revelation of the love of God. Only then will we have the compassion we need to go out and reach our neighbors. It will be this revelation of love that will give us the strength to birth our dreams and change our world.

I used to have great difficulty in talking to others about Jesus because I had no confidence that I was truly loved by God. When I received a revelation about how much my heavenly Daddy loved me, it totally transformed my ability to talk to others about Jesus. Now, if I am sitting next to someone on a plane, walking down the street or shopping, something in me naturally wants to reach out and touch others. I want to tell people about the God who loves me so amazingly. When you understand God's abundant love toward you, you have "too much" love, and you just have to give some away! You cannot keep silent; you have to do what God has called you to do. You push through all the fears, and you begin to birth the dreams of God.

This revelation that we are princes and princesses of our Father is not a self-indulgent thing intended only to make us feel good about ourselves; it is given that it might overflow our lives and touch others. It is meant to release a shout to the world, to show them what true love really looks like. It is the strength that will push us through every limitation; it is the revelation that we need to dream with God. We are His partners in the Kingdom. We are the children of the King, and now our King has given us work to do in the family business—the Kingdom of God. We belong to God, and He has given us everything we need to succeed. So, as we conclude this chapter, speak this word over your life—declare it to every mindset and let a new confidence grow inside that you can do all He has given to you—and you will succeed! Every dream will come to birth. We declare it—now let it be!

##  A prophetic declaration for your life

You carry royal blood and royal destiny in your veins.
You were born into a royal household.
You have been trained for a throne from the moment of birth.
You were born for dignity.
You were born to carry a crown.
He took the crown of thorns, the crown of rejection, so that
you can wear the crown of splendor and acceptance.

You are not an accident.
You were individually and personally handcrafted by the
greatest Creator of all time.
He made you for a purpose and perfectly fitted you for your
function.
If you are ever to truly pray with authority, you must break
the lie of all negativity and walk like a royal child,
comfortable with the crown you were made to wear.

This crown is worn on your head; it covers your mind and
destroys every stronghold of fear and rejection.
You are the child of the King of Kings.
What you feel is not the reality; what is within you—your
dreams and talents and aspirations, your spiritual DNA and
life, all the potential of your yet-unspoken dreams, all your
visions—this is who you truly are.

So let what is hidden on the inside stand up boldly.
Will you not display this in all its majesty to the world?
It is time for the people of God, designed by God, His royal
household, to be revealed, so that everyone can see it.
This is the Esther hour for the Church; it is not a time to
remain silent.

We have been born for such a season; He has prepared us for purpose in this hour.

If we are to fulfill our destiny in this time, we must know who we are and be confident of the royal mandate given into our hands.

We must speak; we must declare; we must lead.

It is time to release our purpose with dignity.

Do not hold back!

We have a royal commission from heaven.

There is a job for us to do.

So, let us stand up boldly, walk with dignity and fulfill our destiny.

We are the royal priesthood of God.

We are the generation of princes and princesses who will take the land.

# SECTION 3

## *Supernatural Breakthrough and Breakout*

# Breakthrough in the Wilderness

## The cry that turns the wilderness

Whatever the task at hand, once there is an army of ordinary people gripped with a vision of change determined to work together to fulfill their dream, we can think the job is virtually done and the breakthrough is imminent. More often than not we find that even with all these criteria fulfilled, there is still more delay and opposition! We discover that although the word of God comes into our lives and we grip that word, we suddenly wake up in the wilderness—a hot, dry place where we have to fight for our dream to be born! It is here that we have to learn to let the supernatural invade the natural and battle for the breakthrough that will bring the change. Now we begin to wrestle with that dream of promise for the season of breakout in our lives, homes and communities.

Isaiah 40:3 is a familiar Bible passage to most of us because it contains the prophetic cry of John the Baptist who later heralded the coming of Jesus: "The voice of one crying in the wilderness: 'Prepare the way of the LORD; make straight in the desert a highway for our God' " (NKJV).

In my life I have often stood clinging to a word of promise and then found myself in a wilderness situation where the word seemed impossible. At such times I have found that a cry needs to come forth from my mouth and break through the heavens to make a way for the dream to be revealed. This verse is precious to me, as it carries a key for breakthrough that God has etched on my spirit. It has been a foundational word, one through which God seems to reveal a new facet of revelation every time I look at it. It is essential that we realize that it is *while we are still in the midst* of a spiritual battle that a cry must come forth. It is when things look bleak and are getting worse, and any breakthrough seems impossible, that the God of the impossible waits to hear our cry.

In 2002 I heard a CD produced by Abundant Life Church in Bradford, England. Knowing the city and the general spiritual climate there, the words of the song impacted me. Bradford has literally been overwhelmed by Islam. In this city the large Methodist church that was once the headquarters of John and Charles Wesley's missions ministry is now an Islamic cultural center. Much of the landscape of the city has lost its passion for Jesus, and it is now godless or celebrates other religions. But in the midst of this barren spiritual landscape came a cry. This church wrote a song in the midst of the wilderness, and the cry said in no uncertain terms:

> "God of miracles, God of the impossible is here,
> God is here. . . . Let the broken-hearted rejoice. . . .
> God is here His wonders to perform."[1]

When we are in the wilderness and things just appear to be getting worse and worse, as the standards of God are being

1. Lara Martin, "God Is Here" (Abundant Life Ministries, Bradford, England). Copyright © 2002 Thankyou Music. Used by permission.

squeezed and put under pressure from every angle, a cry needs to come forth from the wilderness. We need to see things from *a* a different perspective and understand that there is something God wants to release from us that will be *a key to turn the wilderness.* Even though we feel weak in the face of overwhelming circumstances, God is strong. He is the God of the impossible. He can turn the wilderness. God is here and He has the last word. He is the God of wonders.

## Just what is going on?

As we look at the state of our nations, it is easy to become overwhelmed. It seems that darkness is encroaching at every turn. Recently in the United Kingdom, the issue of same-sex marriages being officiated by certain Anglican ministers and the possible appointment of a gay bishop has been foremost on the agenda of outraged Christians. Such things make us think, *How long can this go on? What has happened to the moral fabric of our society?* There is a sense of alarm among many people as they begin to cry, "Just what is going on?"

These feelings of being overwhelmed can move us one *b* of two directions: into a state of hopelessness or into a place of believing to see the supernatural. Recently, as I was once again reading Isaiah 40:3, God spoke to me and said something that stopped me in my tracks: *Rachel, you need to realize that the wilderness is the perfect environment for My miracles to grow.* The impact of the words hit me with force, and I realized that when things look impossible, that is the perfect, most fertile habitat for the God of wonders to work.

We may look at the world and see that it is becoming more and more spiritually barren, but the wilderness is not our major problem; it is not our responsibility, actually, but God's. God can turn the wilderness, but He needs a response of faith from us! To imagine the wilderness becoming a place that is anything other than a parched, dusty, empty, lifeless place may be hard or even impossible for us. But I know a God who takes impossible things and makes them possible. I know a God who takes that which is barren and makes it fruitful. I know a God who takes the desert place and makes a river in its midst. I know a God who takes those who are cursed and makes them blessed. I know a God who takes darkness and makes it light. I know a God who takes the negative and makes it positive. I know a God who takes sin and makes it righteousness. I know a God who takes sickness and makes it health. Do you know that God today?

## Darkness before the light

If you study the historic Church revivals that have taken place down the centuries, you will notice that the chapter of history preceding the revival always seemed to be one on the edge of moral bankruptcy, social injustice, demonic darkness and strife. It seems that the outbreak of revival happens in the midst of a spiritually dead landscape. Out of gross darkness comes an amazing burst of light. When you least expect to see God, He suddenly appears and declares He is still the Light!

In 2004 Christians in the United Kingdom celebrated the centenary of the Welsh revival. The year 1904 saw a dramatic move of God sweep the land. But in 1902 things looked completely different for the Welsh Church. Historic accounts tell us that the superintendent of the Sunday schools in Aberystwyth, Wales, called together all the Sunday school workers in Wales for a conference. As the workers met and talked with one another, the verdict was unanimous: "How can we continue having a ministry to children? They are so unruly that it has become dangerous for women to be alone in the classroom with these children."

A report published at that time described the situation graphically:

> The children are rude; there are brawls happening in the classroom; they are carrying knives; there is fighting; the pews are getting damaged; the hymn books are being ripped up; they are even setting fire to church property. . . . Their language is so vile that we can't allow that sort of blaspheming in the house of the Lord.[2]

Does any of this sound familiar? It sounds to me very much like the report of an inner-city London borough or a downtown school in East Central L.A.

The conclusion of the report was this: They would give it one more year to see if they were able to continue or not. But before the deadline was up, the tide had turned and God had stepped into the Sunday school classes. One of the greatest historic revivals ever had begun.

When we look at our present situation, it is tempting to think, *Things have never been as bad as they are now.* But I have discovered something: It is the same devil at work throughout history, and the devil has not created anything new. God is the Creator, and the devil just perverts what God has made! If you look back through history, you will find the same stinking sin being committed over and over again. The darkness encroaches on society and threatens to overwhelm it, but if the people of God will cry out, then God will step in—and I know a God who can turn the wilderness and make it a field of revival!

While the wilderness is not our problem, it should be our *provocation.* The barren moral decay should cause us to

2. http://www.revival-library.org.

cry out in the midst of this wilderness. The wilderness can actually be transformed in a moment just like Isaiah 35 tells us, but there has to be a trigger point; something has to happen to cause God to turn to our aid. God is waiting to hear our cry.

## Desert warfare

Christians filled with the fire of God are made for desert warfare. We are the Desert Rats Battalion—soldiers specially trained to win in the desert! We are God's special services, equipped for wilderness warfare. God has made us to be wilderness conquerors. But in this day I believe that many of God's soldiers have become overwhelmed by the desolate landscape of the wilderness and have temporarily lost their courage. They have forgotten what the wilderness is there for. When I read in Isaiah 40:3, "Prepare the way of the LORD; make straight *in the desert* a highway for our God" (emphasis added), it stirs me to think that our prayers—our cries to God—form a landing strip for Him in the wilderness. When our heartcry reaches God's ears, it creates a path in the desert so that He can walk right into the heart of the wilderness and make His awesome presence known. It is right in the midst of this nothingness that God will show His hand.

In Isaiah 54:1 we read: "'Sing, O barren woman, you who never bore a child; burst into song, shout for joy, you who were never in labor; because more are the children of the desolate woman than of her who has a husband,' says the LORD." It is while we are still barren and we feel the hopelessness of this condition that we need to make a sound—a sound of hope. In other words, we should sing out not simply when we have the breakthrough, but before it comes; sing while you are still barren! Cry out in the wilderness. Do not wait for something to happen and then speak; speak and make something happen! Yes, it is easy to become discouraged at times, but I believe we have come too far with God on this journey to go back. We have invested too much in our cities and our nations to abandon our investment now. Just because the dividends look poor in this season and it seems there is little return from our investment, do we tear up our share certificates? No, we know we must stick it out for the long haul. In the stock market, things have been pretty rough, but what do you do during a time of poor dividends? You hold, you wait, you watch for change!

Many prayer warriors have invested countless hours in pursuit of God to see a change in our nation, to see God's Kingdom break out. With all this investment, there has been a hope of seeing a rich return. I do not believe that investment has been in vain, and I do not believe that hope has been a false hope. God wants to strengthen our courage and reassure us that He who is coming will come and will not delay. He will visit our nations and reopen the wells of signs, wonders and miracles. I believe our nations will touch, see and know the miraculous power of the living God.

But guess what? The devil does not want to release this to us easily. We need to fight for it. And guess where the Church needs to fight this fight of faith? In the wilderness! Why? This is the environment of the enemy, but we will win because we are the desert rats. Just like Jesus in Luke 4, we are led by the Spirit into the wilderness to battle for our destiny. Wilderness warfare involves the declaration of God's prophetic words and promises that we each carry in our beings. We need to break the "sound barrier" of intimidation with the cry, "It is written!" As we begin to speak these words, they prepare a place for God to come and turn the land back to complete alignment with Him.

## Where is our voice?

If the key to entreating God to act on our behalf is to persistently cry out to Him right in the midst of the desert, then the devil's tactic is to try to shut our mouths. Feelings of helplessness and intimidation shut our mouths; depression shuts our mouths; negativity shuts our mouths. We all succumb to these traps at times, but God wants to hear the voice of His people. He wants to hear our cry in the wilderness—not a sobbing sound of surrender, not a pathetic cry of fear, but a strong prophetic cry of faith declaring that our God is coming! In the Church, there has been a lot of talking from our *souls*, a sound of whining about the circumstances that surround us. Instead this cry needs to come from our *spirits*—a deep prophetic declaration from the depths of our beings, the trigger that begins to turn the wilderness. Although the wilderness is a barren, desolate place, my God loves the challenge of starting from nothing. Just as God chose the natural nation of Israel to be an illustration of a garden carved out in a wilderness, so I believe God wants us, the Church, to spiritually carve out His holy nation from the wilderness of our secular, godless world.

This cry in the wilderness needs to establish the absolutes of God's truth and pull down a plumb line from heaven to earth. It is a cry that confronts the face of the devil. Everything in our society at this time is struggling to be free of the boundaries of right and wrong. People do not want to be told about absolute truth; they do not want a clear distinction between good and evil. We are pressured to be politically correct, to make sure that people feel comfortable and not challenged! All-inclusiveness and "sensitivity" to each individual's personal preference is the order of the day. But my God is the God of the plumb line, the God of boundaries, the God of a clear "yes" and "no," of "shall be" and "shall not be," of black and white.

The cry that comes up from the wilderness has to be in alignment with the cry that comes from heaven. Now is not the time to be declaring our good ideas: "O God, please do this; please do that." We must know the "God idea" and speak it out! The cry that turns the wilderness is the cry that brings earth and heaven into agreement. It is the Kingdom cry that declares, "Let it be on earth as it is already in heaven!" God does not need our suggestions, but He does require our obedience.

The cry that God's people need to learn in these days is the *homologeo* cry. In Greek the word *homo* means "same" and the word *logos* means "word of God." So *homologeo* literally means "to say the same thing as God is saying." This means that when we look at the wilderness, instead of saying, "Oh no, what is going on here? It's a disaster!" we prophesy, speaking the word of God and saying, "God is coming in this place." Instead of agreeing with the wilderness, we agree with heaven, and we say the same thing as God, coming into alignment with Him and His promises. We speak that which heaven speaks and not what our circumstances are shouting!

What is the word that God has deposited in your heart for your city, for your nation? What is the word that He has put in your heart for your church, for your marriage, for your children, for your home? That promise needs to become the sound that comes out of your spirit and echoes back to heaven. This declaration will turn the wilderness, and something will happen!

Paul uses the word *homologeo* several times throughout Romans 10:8–9:

> "The word is near you; it is in your mouth and in your heart,"
> that is, the word of faith we are proclaiming: That if you confess
> [*homologeo*] with your mouth, "Jesus is Lord," and believe in your
> heart that God raised him from the dead, you will be saved.

So many people believe with their heart but then find that the confession of their mouth is out of alignment with what they say they really believe. We may pray and really believe in our heart that our friend is going to be healed of cancer, but then when we begin to talk, we speak a negative report, and our mouth and heart are out of alignment. We believe one thing and confess something different! Perhaps you know that God really loves you—you have understood the revelation of God's great love for you—and yet every time you open your mouth, you speak about how inferior and useless you are and confess that you feel rejected and unloved. Your confession is seriously out of alignment with the truth! If we really want to know the power of God in our life, then we must get our mouth and heart into alignment and begin to speak in agreement with God. We must learn to *homologeo*! We must practice saying the same thing as God in every circumstance.

## Comfort my people

Looking again at the opening verses of Isaiah chapter 40, notice that it begins with a challenge: "Comfort, comfort my people, says your God" (verse 1).

As believers we need to create an atmosphere of godly "comfort" and strengthen and encourage one another with the truth that change *will* come. This is the atmosphere from which the cry in the wilderness should come forth—not out of sheer desperation but with an assurance that God will come to our aid.

As believers we need to comfort one another in the most biblical sense of that word. *Comfort* in the Bible does not carry the soft and fluffy meaning that modern usage has conferred upon it. To comfort a person in the biblical sense is to literally "come [*com*] with strength [*forte*]." In the United Kingdom, "Comfort" is the brand name of a popular fabric softener and is promoted as the essential ingredient to make your towels soft and fluffy when you wash them, but this is not what the Bible means by comfort. God does not want us to have a soft, fluffy experience; He wants us to be strengthened with courage and reinforced in our faith to press on! Instead of commiserating with one another and wallowing in our self-pity, we need to come alongside one another, challenge each other to hang on and give strength to those who are feeling weak.

In the famous Bayeaux tapestry, there is a section entitled "King Harold comforted his troops." When you look more closely at the picture in this section, you see King Harold on his horse with a strong lance in his hand, and he is driving this lance into the backside of one of his soldiers! Over this picture hangs the phrase, "King Harold comforts his men." This is more like the picture of biblical comfort! We need to take courage from the Word of God and use it to inspire one another to press in and keep walking through the difficult times.

When we are truly comforting God's people, we come with this sound of strength, and our horizontal communication is in alignment with our vertical God-communication. We speak faith to each other and we reinforce the Word of God; we affirm the prophetic words that God has given us about our church, our community, our city and our nation, and we hold fast to that which God has said, believing it will come to pass. We need to encourage one another to lift up our heads and put our shoulders back, to regain the sense of dignity and destiny that belongs to a child of God. Truly, your God will come! He will not disappoint you!

## The steel of the Word within you

The steel of the Word of God will keep you from wavering in disbelief when things get tough in the wilderness. God's

Word in us has a similar effect to the steel that reinforces concrete.

Concrete is basically made from dust and water. This is similar to human beings who are also made of 90 percent water plus a bit of dust—the minerals commonly found in the earth. We all think of concrete as a strong material that can carry heavy loads. But is this true? If you make a bridge out of concrete alone and let heavy trucks drive over it, it will collapse. Why? Because concrete on its own does not have the capacity to bear loads and support heavy weights. However, if you insert steel rods into concrete, suddenly all kinds of amazing structures can be built. A steel-reinforced concrete bridge will happily bear the weight of numerous huge trucks for many generations. Steel, dust and water can be brought together to form an incredible combination of strength.

It is the same with people: human "dust and water" alone cannot bear the weight of the destiny we carry within us; our society shows us that. Whenever people make the decision to live their lives independently of others, they soon discover that they cannot cope with the pressures of life and begin to collapse. Many—even those who do have other people to support them—find the stress of life too much to bear and turn to medication to help them. Society possesses thousands who "get by" through living on Prozac and sleeping pills, taking uppers and downers, trying to cope with the pressures of life and generally failing. Dust and water cannot bear the responsibility of life alone! They need reinforcement. Similarly, as believers we need to live with the reinforcement of the Word of God like steel within us. We need to know that it is this Word that will keep us upright and strong in the day of the wilderness. Jesus Himself said in the wilderness, "Man does not live on bread alone, but on every word that comes from the mouth of God" (Matthew 4:4).

As believers standing together and believing for God to break out in our nations, we need to realize we do not have the capacity within us to make this happen. Our faith and strength will fail, so we must learn to lean on and take strength from the Word of God. We will never have the capacity to carry the weight of the prophetic destiny of our communities and homes alone; we will grow weary, but those who wait on the Lord for His word renew their vigor and find fresh reinforcement to stand! That is why we must continually "comfort" one another, declaring and reminding each other of the prophetic word and lifting each other up when we become downhearted. That is why it is so important that we make a priority of gathering together and encouraging one another. This is *not* a time to scatter, with each one of us going to our own little places, but a time to *gather*, when we must come together and speak out encouragement. Like a fire we must keep the coals of prophetic purpose burning, for if we get spread out, it is too easy to extinguish the flames of passion. So resist every temptation to stay isolated, but come together and remember to speak the same things that God is speaking, and exhort one another, "Don't give up now! Our breakthrough is coming. We will see God's Kingdom break out."

## Out of the wilderness

The wilderness is often the place where, because of our vulnerability and brokenness, God is able to take hold of us and use us. When people fall on their faces before God and cry out for His mercy, they usually receive a greater revelation of Him than they had before. As we surrender to God, we come into alignment with Him, and things begin to change.

This is what happened to spark the Argentinean revival that swept across the country and beyond. After a period of crying out to God, suddenly a fresh revelation of His glory was unleashed, and people came into alignment with His will. Once that happened, *boom!* The wilderness was history! We need to change our perspective of the wilderness. The wilderness is the birthing place of our ministry.

Moses came out of the wilderness and became a mighty deliverer who was instrumental in God's plan to set His people free from the tyranny of Egypt.

Joseph came out of the wilderness of the prison to become the leader of Egypt. He had to walk through the restricted place where he never thought his dreams could grow. He traveled through the wilderness of the pit where his brothers tried to murder him, to Potiphar's house where Potiphar's wife tried to seduce him, to the prison where the cupbearer betrayed him and did not remember him. But he came out of the wilderness to fulfill his destiny and save his nation.

David was anointed to be king over the land, executed the amazing defeat of Goliath and then was chased by Saul into the wilderness where he fled for his life. But there came a day when he came out of the wilderness and became the mighty king of Israel, taking his place in the history books of the nations.

Ezekiel was transported in the Spirit to the wilderness where he was instructed to prophesy to a valley of dry bones and saw in his vision the Holy Spirit move in awesome power. What is prophecy? It is declaring the same thing as God! Prophecy is literally the spoken dream of God for your life.

John the Baptist ministered in the wilderness and was the prophetic voice that declared the coming of the Messiah. He said, "Behold! The Lamb of God who takes away the sin of the world!" (John 1:29, NKJV). As Jesus and John the Baptist approached one another for the first time, a transition began to take place. John the Baptist knew that he must now "decrease" because the world was entering the new season of beholding the Lamb. The Kingdom of Heaven had come.

Today I believe we must see the prophetic season finish its task of crying in the wilderness to prepare the way for the next season when the Kingdom of heaven will be revealed on the earth! A transition must take place in the Spirit to usher in this next season, which will release signs, wonders, healings and miracles in our streets, just as it happened with the early Church.

Up to the point where John the Baptist ushered in the season of the Messiah, there had been no mighty miracles in his ministry. John had to work in the wilderness as he prepared a highway for the Lord. He had to call people to repentance, literally to change direction and come into alignment with heaven. When John the Baptist looked up and saw Jesus, he knew the wilderness season was over. A new season had come; the Kingdom of God had arrived. Revival had come, and the miracles began to flow. This will happen for us, too, if we persevere through the wilderness and faithfully prepare a highway for our God.

Too many abandon the struggle in the wilderness just before the point of breakthrough. We decide we have had enough of crying in the wilderness; surely the Kingdom of God should come now? But until He has come, it is *not* time to go! If only we would persevere a little longer! I do not believe that we have yet finished preparing that mighty highway for the coming of God. It is hard work, and there is something in us that cries, "How long, O Lord?" But we need to wait for that moment when we can confidently say, "Behold, God is here."

A couple of years ago, having established the London M25 Prayernet[3] and seen it running well for several years, I began to

3. An extensive prayer network that follows the pattern of the M25 motorway circling Greater London.

think about stepping back from it and letting others with their new initiatives take a lead. Many people had called the initiative "very successful," and it was one of the longest-running prayer ministries of its type. I could fill several hundred pages with story after story about what happened as a result of people gathering together to pray for their city. The praying people of God saw the enemy ambushed time after time.

However, with so many demands on my time, I began to think maybe it was something I should let go of. I tried to convince myself that the job was done. I wanted to release myself from the burden of this wilderness! But then came one of those divine appointments that only God can arrange. I went into London with my daughter to do some shopping. We were looking for her wedding dress and decided to cut through one of the big London stores to get to where we were going. As we did so, I was confronted by a large picture. It was a picture of the Houses of Parliament, our place of government, and the building was painted in gold, red and orange. It looked just as if the building was on fire, just as if the glory of God had impregnated the very stones of the building. Suddenly I was standing in front of this picture, sobbing. I just could not control myself as the Holy Spirit touched something deep within me and asked me some simple questions: *Rachel, does this matter to you? Does your city matter to you? Does My glory matter to you? Then do not let go until you have done your task!* I was so impacted, and again I heard this question: *Rachel, does this matter to you?* In that second I knew the answer: *My God, I never knew how deeply.* To this day when I think about that moment, I feel the tears rise up again.

Standing looking at my picture of the Houses of Parliament on "fire" (I now have it hanging in my living room), I was reminded of the Great Fire of London. In 1666 a fire ripped through the heart of the city, and as destructive as it was, in reality it saved the people of the city from being wiped out by the plague. The Black Death was being carried by rats that infested the gutters and sewers, and it was virtually impossible to root them out and purge the city of the disease. Thousands of people were dying as a result, but as the Great Fire burned, it cleansed the city, literally saving countless Londoners from the plague.

As I thought about this fire, God spoke to me. *There is another plague in your cities now, and it is just as deadly.* The plague of sin has infected London, and it is also rampant in the cities of America. It is carried by the demonic "rats" that are running into homes through the gateways of our televisions, computers and life choices. These rats carry hatred, anger and abuse. Their bite is poisoning people, and millions are dying of the plague in the cities of the West. Oh, how we need a great fire of revival to burn this plague of sin out from our cities!

London matters to me. Righteous government matters to me. I am desperate to see the glory of God and the fire of His presence come upon our parliament. I must see the glory of God and integrity come back into government. If there is one thing I want to give my life for, it is to see national government stirred by God's power! Will you allow God to burden you for your city in a similar way?

## When the mouth of the Lord speaks

Regarding the city of London, I have said to God, "I've come too far to go back. I've invested too much to give up. I will hold; I must see London turn!" I pray that the Lord will give each one of us fresh grace to persevere in our particular situation. Presently we may see only a valley of dry bones, but I believe that a mighty army of ordinary people will arise. Presently we may see the spiritual barrenness of the wilderness, but I believe we will hear the cry that turns this wilderness. Why? Because the mouth of the Lord has spoken it. As we take a final look at our passage in Isaiah 40, we read, "And the glory of the LORD will be revealed, and all mankind together will see it. For the mouth of the LORD has spoken" (verse 5).

We can have confidence in the cry we release from our spirit, because we know this is not our "good idea," but an echo of the words spoken by the mouth of God. Our request has originated in heaven; it is the very cry of God for our city and nation. We will see the glory of God. Why? Because the mouth of the Lord has spoken this. His word always comes to pass. What God speaks will be done. His word never falls to the ground. I believe that God has spoken over the nations and challenged the Church to be His mouthpiece concerning the glory of God. *We have spoken because God spoke first.* This is the cry that will turn the wilderness; this is the sound of breakthrough. We will see the wilderness turn because God has spoken. It will come!

# The Breakthrough Anointing

*"One who breaks open the way will go up before them;*
*they will break through the gate and go out.*
*Their king will pass through before them,*
*the LORD at their head."*

Micah 2:13

As we consider this God of breakthrough, we have to shift our way of thinking. As described in the last chapter, we have definite paradigms that affect our attitudes. When we look at a wilderness, we do not expect to see a garden of flowers but a wasteland of sand. When we look at the United Kingdom, for instance, we do not expect to watch miracles breaking out like popcorn but rather that our prayers for healing will be hindered. We have certain mindsets that have been established over years that control our expectations. So we do not expect to see the extraordinary breakthrough of God in our everyday circumstances. Yet we long for this and are so hungry to see His glory revealed in the Western nations.

We need to know that the wilderness can change, and extraordinary fruit can grow in our desert. Often when I arrive in a city to minister and the pastor meets me at the airport, the conversation will take this turn: "Rachel, we are delighted to have you with us and we are so excited about what God will do, *but* you need to understand that this place is a graveyard for prophets and churches. This is a tough place, and you will probably sense the resistance. We are holding on and trusting, but this is hard ground!" One day after one of these conversations, I was sitting in my hotel room considering this "tough ground," and I felt the Holy Spirit speak to me. *Rachel,* He said, *I can grow anything, anywhere. All I need is the right atmosphere, and you and I can create that together!* As I was considering this statement, I felt God give me a picture. I saw the Eden project in Bodelva, Cornwall, in Southwest England. This project is an amazing botanical feat. Some visionaries built a series of large domes over a large clay pit and planted a garden that would re-create the major elements of the world's floras in England. The fact that the site they used was a china clay pit coming to the end of its working life was part of the miracle. Later these men were heard to say, "It is one thing to build a garden to display the diversity and riches of the world, but doing so in a large, soil-less rainwater sump like Bodelva was probably one of the biggest horticultural challenges ever undertaken." They accepted the challenge to change a wilderness into a garden, and they did it by building domes that changed the local atmosphere so that palm trees and mangoes grew happily in cold England!

God is challenging us to do the same. He is the breakthrough God, and He is challenging us to change the atmosphere around us and bring fruitfulness to the barren ground by our praise and perseverance.

## Time for a breakout of joy

I love the beginnings of the year. I love that January feel, the sense of excitement and anticipation that comes as you wonder

what the year has in store for you. What will God speak this
year, and what will break through the barren ground? I
remember one year Gordon being so enthusiastic to embrace
the new year that early on January 1, he jumped out of bed,
saying, "Right, Christmas is done; let's find the new challenge,"
and immediately set about dismantling the Christmas tree and
decorations. I thought, *This man is on a mission!* He was carrying
the sense that God has spoken promises over our lives, and here
was a new season unfurling; we had the opportunity to seize
the day and watch what God had said begin to happen.

Each new year is a gift from God, and you never know quite
what He will do in your life in any year. But there are also
"seasons in the Spirit" when it appears that a word from God is
released corporately and influences the whole Church or a
nation. Several people have expressed that they felt 2005 was
a year of wrestling and struggling to see the word of God break
through for them. Prophetically it was a time when, although
people's spiritual goals were clear, they had to fight to achieve
them, and at times the goalposts seemed to be constantly
moving. All over the United Kingdom we found people using
the word *breakthrough*, and we sensed that this was the cry in
the Church. Maybe you have felt this cry, too. Perhaps you
have a clear, God-given vision for your ministry, and yet
finance is constantly a challenge. Maybe your relationships
with others have been put under surprising pressure, and you
had to struggle to watch the promise of God become reality,
knowing that the "mouth of the Lord" had spoken it.

Whatever your struggle has been, prophetically I believe that
we are coming into a season of breakthrough where we will see
a *breakout* of joy as many of these hindrances and barriers are
removed. You can sense when there is a change in the spiritual
atmosphere, when you are moving out of one season and into
another. This new season will be as different as a butterfly is to

a caterpillar (see the illustration in chapter 2). A butterfly is able to move in a completely different dimension than a caterpillar. The latter is earthbound, whereas the former can fly freely— but they are essentially the same creature in a different form! There is a season of struggle in the Spirit whenever anything worthwhile is birthed, but eventually there comes the break-out—a breakthrough into a boundless and unconstrained environment. There is a breakout coming for many.

Over recent years, some of us have felt like caterpillars trying to find our butterfly wings. We have been constrained, held in and limited. But the time of breakout is coming. I believe for many this next season will be one of new things—"out of the box" new. But it will also be a season of completion, of finishing things that we have already begun.

In this last season, some have been struggling with their own identity—to understand who they really are in Christ, to grasp hold of their significance and their destiny. There has been a wrestling and a struggling against the intimidation and fear of the enemy. He's eyeballed you and said, "You're nothing." It simply is not true. In this coming season, you are going to wrestle through that and win. There will be a breakout of faith so that you know, beyond doubt, that you are a new creation. God will give you the breakthrough so that you have a new sense of significance, and that will transform your whole understanding of yourself.

In Micah 2:13 we read this: "One who breaks open the way will go up before them; they will break through the gate and go out. Their king will pass through before them, the LORD at their head."

You are equipped to break out and break through because your incredible Jesus is with you every step of the way. He's broken through before you and paved the way for you. He has broken through so that you can break through! You can live in the experience of Jesus' victory. That is your heritage in Him. But what exactly does it mean to break out? What is the full biblical picture of breakthrough and breakout?

## What is breakout?

Like many Bible expositors, when I begin to think about a word, I like to find the full breadth and depth of its biblical meaning. So I usually type the word into my computer to see what my Bible software suggests. The Hebrew word *parats* is used 49 times in the Bible, and "to break out" is its core meaning, though it is not translated that way. *Parats* (pronounced "poor rats") carries the sense of breaking out in every context; in fact, it is applied directly, indirectly, literally and figuratively. The definitions of *parats* hardly seem able to describe just how deep and wide is this breakout that the Bible is trying to communicate to us! It means the following: to cut abroad, to break away, to break down, to be a breaker, to break through, to break in, to break up, to break forth, to come apart, to spread out, to go abroad, to compel, to disperse, to grow, to increase, to open up, to press in, to scatter, to urge. It is an incredibly expansive word; this breakout is in every possible direction, and we lose much of its sense of enormity in our English Bible translations.

## Where will this breakout occur?

As we study the Scriptures, we find that there are many places where this word *parats* is used, although the English translation does not always use the term "break out." But if we trace this word, it gives us a clue about the areas God targets with this breakthrough anointing. We find it is a consistent theme throughout Scripture, and so we discover that God really is the God of breakthrough!

## 1. Breakout against our enemies

Second Samuel 5:20 says, "So David went to Baal Perazim, and there he defeated them. He said, 'As waters break out, the LORD has broken out against my enemies before me.' So that place was called Baal Perazim."

There are seasons in your life when you break out, and you know that a particular enemy that has confronted you for many years has been defeated. Maybe the enemy of anger has dogged your life for a long time, but there came a moment of breakout when you knew, *That's it! I've broken through! It's finished.* Like David, who was pursued by the Philistines many times, there came a time when it was finished, and he knew he had defeated them; at last he lived in peace for his generation. It is the same with us; there comes a moment when you know the enemy of your yesterday has been defeated and you have broken out and are free. The breaker's anointing has broken the stronghold of the enemy in your life.

## 2. Breakout of territory

Isaiah 54:2 says, "Enlarge the place of your tent, stretch your tent curtains wide, do not hold back; lengthen your cords, strengthen your stakes."

Our God designates boundaries and territory. He likes to settle His people in a particular place to do a specific job. God gives you a place and says, "This is your land; this is your turf— own your geography." Then He gives you influence over that territory—an authority so that you can actually do what you are called to do. We see this in Isaiah 54:3, where we read, "You will spread out [*parats*] to the right and to the left; your descendants will dispossess nations and settle in their desolate cities." God wants to give us a breakout anointing so that we can be people of influence in our geography.

### 3. Breakout of wealth and possessions

Job 1:10 says, "Have you not put a hedge around him and his household and everything he has? You have blessed the work of his hands, so that his flocks and herds are spread throughout [*parats*] the land."

There comes a time when God decrees a breakout of wealth and prosperity upon His people. The phrase "to the right and to the left" means you are surrounded by God's blessing. You simply cannot avoid it! Often we have felt that the godlier we are, the poorer we should be, but God's way is different. He wants His people to experience a breakout of blessing both financial and spiritual, not either/or! Again, in Genesis 30:43, which refers to Jacob, we read, "In this way the man grew exceedingly [*parats*] prosperous." Here the "exceedingly" signifies a breakout of prosperity—a wide, expansive, all-encompassing, unprecedented prosperity! Often we battle for the financial release for our projects and lives, but God wants us to experience a breakout of supernatural provision.

### 4. Breakout of numbers and people

In Genesis 28:14 God reminds Jacob of the promise He made to Abraham, his grandfather:

> "Your descendants will be like the dust of the earth, and you will spread out [*parats*] to the west and to the east, to the north and to the south. All peoples on earth will be blessed through you and your offspring."

When God causes you to break out, you are not only blessed today, but you are able to leave a legacy of blessing in the land for the next generation, too. This breakout anointing affects generations and leaves favor and blessing as an inheritance. It also means that God will bless your family line and give you sons and daughters and increase your numbers. I also believe that this is a season when many of us will see our spiritual sons and daughters born and then watch them spread out into our communities and cites with their love for Jesus breaking through.

### 5. Breakout of birthing

Genesis 38:29 says, "But when he drew back his hand, his brother came out, and she said, 'So this is how you have broken out [*parats*]!' And he was named Perez."

This unusual story occurred during a time of barrenness, difficulty and struggle. Tamar, who became pregnant through tragic circumstances, finally gave birth to twins. But it was not an easy birth! There was some struggling and wrestling before the breakout of birth finally came. I believe many of us have been through seasons of betrayal and difficulty, but if we will allow the season to mature, there will be a double blessing born out of that time. We will give birth to twins, and the breaker's anointing will break though all the circumstances and bring life into a barren area of our lives.

### 6. Breakout of multiplication in the season of difficulty

The book of Exodus tells of the oppression of the people of Israel and how they were pushed down and suppressed. They were living in a land where they were working extremely hard but getting very little in return. They were forced into slavery and ridiculed for their faith. Everyone made it hard for them to be who they were: a people of destiny with an identity in the land. They were mocked and enslaved. Does that sound a bit familiar? Have you gone through trials for your faith because your family does not understand your God? Have you been mocked and ridiculed by your work colleagues? Society wants to silence the people of God because it rejects the truth about Jesus. People cannot even stand to hear His name spoken with affection because they do not want their selfish comfort zones to be disturbed.

Yet, it says in Exodus 1:12, "The more they were oppressed, the more they multiplied and spread [*parats*]; so the Egyptians came to dread the Israelites."

The more the Israelites were oppressed, the more they broke out! Their Egyptian masters must have thought, *What can we do with these people? The more we try to put them in a box, the more they spill out everywhere. The more we try to contain them, the more they grow! The more we try to make them impoverished, the richer they get! What can we do?* They came to dread the uncanny ability of the people of God to keep breaking out. The breakout factor is still part of our DNA as the people of God! It puts fear and terror into the heart of the enemy. He knows he cannot contain it. We see this story repeated in China today. Communism said it would kill Christianity and eradicate faith. All the churches were closed and the missionaries were expelled, but God kept breaking out! As we read the amazing stories that come out of China, we realize God is still breaking out today, and all the ridicule and oppression cannot hold Him back.

### 7. Breakout of holiness

In a season of breakout, it is important that we keep our hearts right before God—that we keep in line with His will. Exodus 19:22 says, "Even the priests, who approach the LORD, must consecrate themselves, or the LORD will break out [*parats*] against them."

These are not the days to play games with God. As we cry out for breakthrough, we need to know that God will break out against us if we do not keep His principles. I do not want God against me; I want God for me! A season of breakout is a two-way street. We have to make sure we are living a holy life where God is the King, leading us in breakout, rather than having God's hand opposing us with *His* breakout of anger against our hypocrisy.

### 8. Breakout of the Word

This word *parats* is also used to describe a breakout of God's Word. We see this in 1 Samuel 3. The nation of Israel was in a mess with no godly leadership, and the prophetic voice needed for spiritual direction was silent. The people were lost and directionless, and society had lost the fear of the Lord. Everything was disintegrating. It sounds like a description of present-day Western society! Into this atmosphere came a boy, Samuel, chosen by God to be His voice. Verse 1 (KJV) says, "And the child Samuel ministered unto the LORD before Eli. And the word of the LORD was precious in those days; there was no open [*parats*] vision."

There was no breakout revelation in the land until Samuel was raised up by God to be His mouthpiece. Similarly, we desperately need a breakout of revelation in our nation today—a breakout of the prophetic word for our government and people in places of authority. Our society is being deafened by the sounds of so many voices from different religious communities, but the voice of Jesus—the voice above all other voices—needs to break out and be heard by the nations at this time.

### 9. Breakout season

Most of us are familiar with Ecclesiastes 3:1, which says, "There is a time for everything, and a season for every activity under heaven." But verse 3 says that there is "a time to kill and a time to heal, a time to tear down [*parats*]." The same Hebrew word for breakout is used again. There is a time to break out and a time to build up. I believe we need to pray for this season of *parats*—a time to break out—because it is time to see change come and time to watch our dreams birthed; it is time for the promises of God to break out in our nations once again. There is a time—O God, let this be the time for our nation!

## Holding on for the breakthrough

If you are desperate to see a breakthrough in a particular area in your life or ministry, then take heart because God is faithful and this time will surely come. We must remember that He is the King who leads us. He's at the head; He's the One who walks out; He's the God of the breakout who will help you to break through at the right time.

As we wait for this season of breakthrough, we are often tempted to try every new thing going, hoping that somehow the activity will trigger the long-awaited breakthrough. But we need to realize that so often it is just our consistency and simple obedience that opens the door of breakthrough. Little keys open big doors! It is the simple acts we do that break the stranglehold, not our good ideas. You have to make a decision to finish the tasks you know God has given you, rather than looking for something new. Jesus was an awesome finisher. He completed His task. In the West we tend to be great initiators but very poor finishers. We start well but lose momentum. We see visions and have dreams but abandon the building site when the pressure of building our dreams gets tough!

Recently as I was thinking about the qualities that help us finish successfully, I heard a radio interview with a lady who had run a number of marathons. She said there are two essential skills you need to run a successful marathon. I believe that we can apply these same principles to our spiritual race. Understanding them will help us complete the distance and keep strong while we are waiting for our breakout moment.

## 1. Make sure that you have the finish line in the "right" place

This lady said that when she ran her first marathon, she thought the distance she had to run was just 26 miles (it is actually 26.2 miles). She trained hard for this precise distance, and when she came to run the race she kept her eye on the distance markers. When she reached the 25.6-mile marker, she thought, *Okay, I know I can sprint the rest and finish*, so she began to speed up. Of course, when she reached the 26-mile marker, there was no finish line and no tape! The finish line was still 0.2 miles away. She recalled that by the time she reached the *actual* finish line, she felt like dying because she had begun sprinting way too soon. She commented, "I don't even remember finishing. I think I threw up. I have no memory of the end because I put the tape in the wrong place in my mind!"

If, mentally, you have a wrong perception about the finish line for a season in your life, then you, too, will have an attitude of finishing prematurely. When that happens, it robs you of the joy of going the distance and finishing strong. I see this happen in the Church. We try to force God's hand in order to reach the finish line before it is time. When we are waiting for a financial breakthrough, we set a deadline in our minds: *If God has not supplied the money by this date, then we are finished!* We say, "God, it has to finish here! I asked for this thing in 2006, and You didn't do it—now it's 2007!" But God's ideas about timing rarely coincide with ours! Plus, thinking that God has failed to meet "our deadline" can leave us feeling bitter and disillusioned so that we lose the joy of celebration when the actual breakthrough comes—all because we drew a line somewhere where God did not. Instead of doing this, we need to keep trusting God and keep on running our race to the end. Then we will know the extraordinary joy of a mission accomplished because we have done it—we have finished and broken through.

### 2. The skill of running a long race is a mind game

This lady also said that most people have the body and the physical ability to run 26.2 miles if they are prepared to train for it, but that what separates those who would like to run a long-distance race and those who actually do it is their mental determination. Marathon running is as much about the mind as it is about the body.

Technically, I expect she's correct. If we really wanted to, most people would be physically able to train for and run a marathon (even if it was very, very slowly!). But how many would be prepared to go through the mental stress of blocking out the pain and deciding to push their body way beyond its normal levels of endurance? There comes a point when you depend on the raw courage of your will and mind.

Equally, running your spiritual race and holding on for a breakthrough is a mind game. We often have to battle with the intimidation, doubt and fear that is thrown at us by the enemy. He constantly whispers, "You can't do it; you'll never make it! You'll never finish; you're no good!" But it is a mind game, and we need courage. What he is saying is not the truth. But this battle for our faith rages in our minds. If we are going to experience consistent breakthrough in our lives, then we must win this mind game. Even when we fail and feel overwhelmed, we must realize that God never sends us back to the start to begin our race all over again. No! When we falter or fall, He waits for us to get up, dust ourselves off, carry on running and finish our course. God says to us, "Get up and finish the race, and you will break through. I've given you a promise: You will break out. You have been made to overcome, not to be overwhelmed!"

## Breaking mindsets that hinder the supernatural

If we are going to see a release of the supernatural in signs and wonders in the West, then I believe we must allow God to do some deep brain surgery and challenge our ways of thinking! We need not just a few minor adjustments to our attitudes but a complete overhaul. God wants to *offend* our minds to reveal our strongholds! I believe He wants us to have such a radically different mindset that it bears no resemblance to the way in which most of us think today. He wants us to become childlike again, and He will teach us His ways.

Recently God spoke to me and said that He had a serious issue with the way in which much of the Church thinks. He is not pleased with the vanity of our minds, our intellects, our theology and our inclination to process and criticize everything that is presented to us. He has an issue with our obsession with knowledge over godly wisdom. In the Western Church, we seem to think that we know better than God much of the time! We think we know how everything works. We want to analyze, reason and figure everything out to the extent that the supernatural has been sidelined and canceled out. The result has been that most of our churches are experiencing a famine of the miraculous because we have arrogantly exalted our minds above the expression of the Spirit.

I see the effects of this underlying mindset quite clearly as I minister in different places. So often people will come and say to me, "God has really spoken to me today; now I need to go home and *process* it and see what I think." Part of me longs to reply, "No! Whatever you do, *don't process it* with your mind;

let your spirit respond!" It is precisely this approach of needing to understand everything before we acknowledge the power of God that so limits His supernatural working in our nations.

If you talk to any African, Indian or South American minister who has established a church in their nation, they will invariably have seen numerous signs and wonders. The miraculous is one of God's tools for blasting through the walls of resistance to the Gospel. Where the spiritual landscape looks bleak, resistant and impenetrable, signs and wonders provide the breakthrough and open the door to the message of the cross. The miraculous is the foundation of so much of the worldwide Church, but not so in the West.

In Matthew 10:7–8, we read the exhortation Jesus gave to all would-be disciples:

> "As you go, preach this message: 'The kingdom of heaven is near.' Heal the sick, raise the dead, cleanse those who have leprosy, drive out demons. Freely you have received, freely give."

This is still the same message that we should carry today. But do we mirror the activities of those early disciples? When Jesus and His disciples proclaimed the Kingdom of heaven was near, the sick were healed, the dead were raised and many more miracles took place. Our proclamation of the Kingdom today should carry no less power. We, too, are commissioned to heal the sick, to set captives free from their addictions, to raise the dead. The Bible does not say, "Heal the sick, except for where there is an adequate health care system." It does not say, "Pray for healing—but only when the doctors can't do anymore." We process things too much. We try to define the power of the Holy Spirit and put it into an easily understandable package instead of allowing ourselves to be like lightning conductors between heaven and earth. Our job is to preach the Gospel and to bring heaven down to invade earth. Just like the first disciples, because of our relationship to Jesus we have the ability to bridge the gap between heaven and earth.

## Transforming our minds

Romans 12:1–2 challenges these very issues. Paul writes:

> Therefore, I urge you, brothers, in view of God's mercy, to offer your bodies as living sacrifices, holy and pleasing to God—this is your spiritual act of worship. Do not conform any longer to the pattern of this world, but be transformed by the renewing of your mind. Then you will be able to test and approve what God's will is—his good, pleasing and perfect will.

In verse one Paul "urges" us to comply with his command. In the Greek the word translated "urge" is a strong word, having the same root as "urgent" (*psistis*). Paul's "urgent" command is that we surrender our bodies to God as living sacrifices. Our "body" in biblical thinking includes our mind, our intellect. If we understand this, then verse two makes much more sense. God wants us to put our minds on His altar, not just our bodies, and to surrender our former ways of thinking to Him. So many people refuse to allow God to engage their mind, thinking He is only interested in their heart. Their soul and spirit is engaged with God, but they hold back from letting God transform their thinking, keeping that area of their life protected from all spiritual influence. When this happens, their minds become mere spectators, instead of participators, concerning the things of God. Instead of allowing God to reshape the way they think, they prefer things to be safe and contained.

Have you ever visited another nation where God is moving and been amazed by the fact that miracles just happen routinely? Why is this? I believe it is because they are living under a different heaven! In the West, we live under a blanket of intellectual arrogance. Our limited mindset restricts us from experiencing the glory and supernatural power of God. We need to realize that there is a link between our intellectual pride and our lack of the miraculous. So if you want to carry power in the Kingdom of God and be a person who sees signs and wonders, then you are going to have to let your spirit teach your mind. You will also have to contend with the criticism of those who are entrenched in a completely different mindset. They will probably persecute you and ridicule you. But when the breakthrough eventually comes, those same people are going to be challenged by the miracle. I urge you, offer your mind to God! Put everything to do with your life on His altar. Give it up! It does not mean it is all going to be destroyed; God wants to use your mind and give you supernatural intelligence! But do not let your limited worldview cap the flow of God's supernatural power in your life. Let the supernatural power of God break through!

## Our thoughts are not God's thoughts

Isaiah 55:8–9 says,

> "For my thoughts are not your thoughts,
>    neither are your ways my ways,"
>                   declares the LORD.
> "As the heavens are higher than the earth,
>    so are my ways higher than your ways
>    and my thoughts than your thoughts."

We know these verses so well and recognize their truth and yet we still do not realize how different God's way is. We do not acknowledge that God thinks in an *entirely different* way from us—that His way of thinking is so radically removed from ours that it bears hardly any resemblance at all!

During my life God has really challenged me over the issue of trying to reason with His judgment. We are not equal with God. God's logic is not our logic. What seems perfectly reasonable to us is not right to God, and vice versa! Often when we get frustrated with God, it has to do with what I call the "time-eternity conflict." In other words, God sees the end from the beginning, so He never panics because He knows what is coming. But every day matters to us. We panic and fret about God's timing and think we know when it is time for Him to act. God said to me one day, *Rachel, you need to understand that your thoughts are not My thoughts. But, if you are willing, I can teach you to begin to think like Me.* God *can* cause us to think more like Him, but it is a supernatural thing. No one thinks like God naturally.

Sometimes God moves in ways that are hard to explain. We would like to come up with a working formula to help us always predict what God will do—but we cannot! God never changes, but the way in which He moves to answer prayer is diverse and multifaceted. He likes doing new things. God does not want us to waste our time trying to figure out His methods, because we will never do it. Instead God wants us to seek His face, listen to His voice, obey Him and discover the method for *this time*!

How do we do this? First, we need to get back to the Bible and remind ourselves of what it teaches. We must stop trying to explain away the miracles and accept them. We must stop trying to make our Christian faith politically correct and get back to the fundamentals of our miracle-working God—a God who longs to intervene in our everyday lives. We will never convert people by only going head to head with them and reasoning things out on a solely intellectual level, because the god of this age has blinded their minds (see 2 Corinthians 4:4). People's minds are closed to truly understanding the things of God. The enemy has done that, but he cannot shut down people's spirits. We need to be functioning in the supernatural power of God to break through into people's lives and see a transformation.

My husband, Gordon, once worked with a former Muslim, the son of a mullah, who had given his life to Christ. He was from a very wealthy Kuwaiti family and had been well educated. He was trained in media and television and before being saved was working for a company coordinating satellite telecommunications into North Africa. His mission was to spread the message of Islam across the whole of North Africa through media and television.

While still an ardent Muslim this man visited London, and as he walked down a London road, a YWAM girl approached him and told him that Jesus loved him and could give him peace. Immediately, he was incensed and started shouting at this YWAMer, ranting and raving about the evils of Christianity. The two became locked in an intellectual argument. It was then, however, that the young woman from YWAM received a word of wisdom from God. She said to the man, "Don't fight with me about what I consider to be true. Why don't you ask God for yourself?" Those words penetrated the heart of this militant Muslim. He went back to his hotel room and found a Gideon Bible in his bedside drawer. He looked in the index at the front and noticed there was a series of sections, each with a list of verses underneath for further reading. As he looked at this list, one section jumped out at him—verses to read under the heading: "If you want peace." This man had a hole inside of him. He was desperate for peace. He looked up the first Scripture and began to read. God had gotten him! God spoke to this man. Later he had a dream and a vision in which Jesus appeared to him. Today he uses his media training to spread the Gospel of Jesus!

We can spend too much time trying to package our Gospel message to make it trendy and sophisticated. But the fact is, people's minds are spiritually closed. We need to bypass these intellectual arguments and find the entrance straight to people's hearts, using God's supernatural power expressed through the gifts of the Spirit, especially the gifts of words of knowledge, wisdom and prophecy.

## Being radical for a breakthrough

There is a deep cry in me that says, "Enough is enough!" I have watched enough dear people die of cancer and other terminal diseases. It is time to see them live! We may have to take some risks and do things that will appear extreme or even stupid to others, but we must break through into miraculous power.

If you look back into Church history and read the stories of the great healing evangelists like Smith Wigglesworth and the Jeffrey brothers, you will find that they did some outrageous things at the prompting of the Holy Spirit—things that we still find shocking and extreme today. Yet God moved in awesome power in answer to their obedience. One particular story stands out in my mind as an illustration of their courage to obey.

In his book *Smith Wigglesworth: Apostle of Faith*, author Stanley Howard Frodsham recounts how Wigglesworth raised a woman from the dead in response to the Holy Spirit's prompting. The incident is retold in Wigglesworth's own words:

> My friend said, "She is dead." He was scared. I have never seen a
> man so frightened in my life. "What shall I do?" he asked. You

may think that what I did was absurd, but I reached over into the bed and pulled her out. I carried her across the room, stood her against the wall and held her up, as she was absolutely dead. I looked into her face and said, "In the name of Jesus, I rebuke this death." From the crown of her head to the soles of her feet her whole body began to tremble. "In the name of Jesus, I command you to walk," I said. I repeated, "In the name of Jesus, in the name of Jesus, walk!" and she walked.[1]

What an astonishing miracle! I wonder how many of us would have been audacious enough to have attempted such a thing. I have to ask myself if I would have the guts to pull a dead person out of his or her bed with a grieving relative next to me. Would I refuse to let go until God brought him or her back to life? Or would I crumble and apologize to the horrified onlooker? Today we need men and women of faith who are prepared to really go for it—to hear God clearly and then stick their necks out to believe Him to do incredible things.

## Breaking the strongholds of the mind

What Wigglesworth did was just the kind of thing that Jesus did in His ministry. Jesus Himself once commanded a young man to come back to life, and he sat up in his coffin right in the middle of his own funeral procession (see Luke 7:13–15). Why do we not expect God to empower us to do similar things today? Partly, I believe, it is the fear of stepping out, of taking a risk in case we look foolish or really offend those who are grieving. And partly it is because we are just so entrenched in a mindset that excludes the miraculous—or, at the very least, tells us that it cannot possibly happen *here*.

1.  Stanley Howard Frodsham, *Smith Wigglesworth: Apostle of Faith* (Springfield, Mo.: Gospel Publishing House, 1948) 58–59.

But 2 Corinthians 10:3–4 says, "Though we live in the world, we do not wage war as the world does. The weapons we fight with are not the weapons of the world. On the contrary, they have divine power to demolish strongholds."

God wants us to realize that we have divine power to demolish strongholds. What are these strongholds? Paul gives us the answer in the next verse: "We demolish arguments and every pretension that sets itself up against the knowledge of God, and we take captive every thought to make it obedient to Christ" (verse 5).

Paul suggests that arguments, pretensions and thoughts that are opposed to God will resist the flow of His Spirit. Are there areas in your life where you are arguing with God? Perhaps God is calling you to act upon His word, but you are trying to debate the matter with Him: "Oh, I don't think it's the right time for that..." Every place where you find you are disagreeing with God in your life, demolish it! Every excuse that is in conflict with the call of God, challenge it! Confront every reaction that is contrary to God's word: fear, embarrassment, self-consciousness—everything that stops us from obeying and stepping out in faith to see the supernatural.

We need to tear down every shred of unbelief in our lives. Sometimes people say to me, disparagingly, "Are you a *faith* person?" (referring to the word-of-faith movement within the Church). I generally respond, "God help you if you're not!" What do we have if we do not have faith? Doubt and unbelief! Without faith it is impossible to please God, so I would rather be a faith person than not. I believe one of the things Europe in particular needs to repent of is our mockery of the faith movement. I do not like its excesses, but unfortunately we have thrown out the baby with the bathwater. The faith movement does have something—it challenges our understanding of the divine revelation of the power of faith and the supernatural. Africa embraced the faith movement; the Far East has heard it; and you can see what it has done for the people and the churches there. They are people of faith who know how to stand, persevere and smash through spiritual opposition when necessary. The Bible is a book of faith. It is faith from beginning to end. Unless you believe, you cannot receive! We must pull down the stronghold of unbelief.

So many Christians have this equation in their mind regarding unbelief and faith: unbelief plus the Holy Spirit equals faith. They think that somehow God will come upon our unbelief and help us to reach a place of faith. It is not true. God hates unbelief. He has no time for it. He wants us to pull it down and destroy it. There is no relationship between unbelief and faith. They are polar opposites. One cannot be converted into the other. Unbelief must be removed from our life, while faith is a gift to be received from God. I hate the spirit of unbelief and the religious atmosphere that has swamped our nations. They rob us of our destiny.

First Corinthians 2:14 says, "The man without the Spirit does not accept the things that come from the Spirit of God, for they are foolishness to him, and he cannot understand them, because they are spiritually discerned."

Too many of us make the mistake of trying to use our minds to understand the Spirit of God. We want to understand what the Spirit reveals to us so that we can accept it as truth. But the Bible points out that these spiritual truths are first explained to the spirit, then the mind is educated from the spirit. The fact is, we may never fully understand with our minds the truth we know in our spirits. People always want to process things before they will accept them, but that is not the way in which God works! A spiritual person discerns things by the Spirit of God. Truth cannot always be understood intellectually, but it is discerned and revealed. We must stop trying to control and contain things with our mind. Instead we need a Spirit-controlled mind—one that is led by God's Spirit.

We live in urgent days. God cannot always wait for our minds to catch up with our spirits—we just need to trust His voice and respond. A day is coming when God's Spirit will come upon us and we will have to go with the flow immediately without rationalizing. We must grasp the urgency of the times we live in. People are dying while we are fussing around, trying to analyze God.

## Just do what the Holy Spirit tells you to do!

A few years ago I was in France near the northern border of Belgium. Twelve churches in that region had called their people together, about 1,200 in all, and they met in the largest hall in a central location. As people began to come into that building for the first meeting, I noticed some began to cry. It was because they had not realized there were so many Spirit-filled Christians in that area, and it overwhelmed them!

As I stood to speak, God gave me a specific prophetic sign to demonstrate to these churches that the harvest in Europe was ready and that we live in urgent days. The twelve pastors of the twelve churches were all present at the meetings, and God told me to call each one of them forward and have them turn around toward the congregation, holding their arms out like a basket. The Lord said, *I am going to give every one of you pastors a harvest this morning.* So I asked the twelve pastors to come forward, but I was disappointed to see that only nine responded. I waited and asked again, and then a third time, but still only nine pastors came forward. Without preaching and with just a simple explanation, I went straight into giving an altar call. I just knew that people were going to get saved that morning. I said to the people, "There are those here who need

Jesus today. You've come because there is an aching and a longing inside you. You do not know Jesus as your Lord. But there are men here [I pointed to the pastors] who stand as representatives of Jesus for you. Come right now and give your life to Jesus."

People began to come forward. Amazingly, one person came to each of the nine pastors. Nine people gave their lives to Christ. That was wonderful, but I thought to myself sadly, *What about the other three? What would have happened if those three other pastors had been obedient to God's word?* I knew that there were three more lives that should have been saved in that place, and it really bothered me. This was my last meeting, but the leaders persuaded me to stay on for one more day and to do a final meeting for them on the following Monday night. That evening as I got up to speak, before I had given any kind of altar call, two men came forward—an older and a younger man. As I looked at them inquiringly, one said to me, "I just had to come forward. I know I need to respond." I asked if he had been in the meeting that first morning and he replied, "Yes, but I just couldn't get out of my seat. I couldn't bring myself to come forward then, but I haven't been able to sleep since. I had to come tonight and give my life to Jesus."

The two men were father and son. They had both been on drugs for years. At the previous meeting, they had walked into that place inwardly crying out to God to help them. At that meeting, God met with them and released them from their addictions. From that moment on they had not used drugs, nor had they felt the need to. This evening they had come forward to give their lives to Christ.

Instinctively I knew that these two men were two of the three people who should have responded previously, making twelve in all—one for each pastor of each church gathered together, symbolic of the waiting harvest. *There is still one left, Lord*, I prayed. *Who is it?* Just then an old lady rose from her seat and also came out to the front.

Later when I inquired about the reason the other pastors had not come forward, I was told that they did not feel it was necessary for them to stand at the front, and they were uncomfortable, so they had decided to remain seated. God will ask us to do unusual and maybe even "uncomfortable" things for Him, but we must remember this is not about us; it is about the harvest!

## A demonstration of God's power

At times I feel so inadequate because I am desperate to see God move in power in such a great way, and yet I know I am powerless to make it happen myself! Like Paul, I want to be able to say, "My message and my preaching were not with wise and persuasive words, but with a demonstration of the Spirit's power, so that your faith might not rest on men's wisdom, but on God's power" (1 Corinthians 2:4–5).

As messengers of the Gospel, we cannot allow people's faith to rest on our ability to entertain them with words. I do not want people to remember my words alone; I want them to remember a demonstration of God's awesome power. I want the words I preach to be written on people's lives by the finger of God, imprinted on their spirits. I cannot do that. Only God can.

The great Indian leader Gandhi, who was brought up and educated in Christian schools, once held up the Bible and declared, "If Christians would really live according to the teachings of Christ, as found in the Bible, all of India would be Christian today."[2] Is the Bible just literature to us—just our

2.  http://en.proverbia.net/citastema.asp?tematica=1009.

bedtime story or our morning newspaper? The Bible is so much more and has to be acted upon, not just read.

The following story about an event that happened in Norway challenges us to act, not just speak, and to allow God to break the ungodly mindsets that hold us back. Craig, from Pensacola, Florida, had been sent by his church to help inspire the youth work of a Norwegian church. The current youth pastor was struggling as he saw many of his young people losing their way. Norway has a high suicide rate among 18- to 25-year-old men, and many have turned to drugs as a way of escape. But the tragic death of a backslidden boy who belonged to this youth group ignited a new desperation in the church to see a breakthrough with their young people.

Craig began to work with them, and they organized an evangelistic campaign in the area designed to bring more young people into the church. On one particular Sunday night, nineteen young people came into the meeting. They had cigarettes, beer cans and radios with them. As they came in they continued smoking and drinking and then put their feet up on the pews and turned their radios on! They did everything they could to be disruptive. Craig said to God, "Okay, now what do I do?" and the Holy Spirit spoke to him, saying, *It's time for the Elijah challenge.*

So Craig spoke boldly to these youths, pointing at the ring leader. "You," he said, "are sitting there saying, 'There is no God and there is no power.' I tell you, there is a God and He has power." Then he challenged someone in the group to step forward and say to his face, "There is no God and He has no power."

"If nothing happens," said Craig, "you can take my Bible and do with it what you like. I'll never get another one because you'll have proven it isn't true. In fact, you can have this building as well! There is no point in it being a church if God isn't here. You've got nowhere to go, so you can have it for your gatherings!" It was an offer too good to refuse. One of the nineteen young people rose to the challenge and came to the front. This young guy got right in Craig's face and said, "There's no God!" Craig responded, "There is a God and He has p—"

Craig only managed to get the "p" of "power" out and then *bang!* The young man, without being touched by anyone in the building, was thrown about fifteen feet backward down the center aisle of the church! He lay on the floor, shaking, and did not get up. What happened next? Cigarettes went out, beer cans were put down and radios were turned off. These young people were terrified. They were not sure whether their friend was still alive or whether God had killed him—and none of them were going to get out of their seats to look in case the same thing happened to them! Craig boldly preached the Gospel, and then he told the young man to get up and come to the front. Under the convicting power of the Holy Spirit, he came forward, saying, "Jesus, please save me!"

If we are going to run this race and see the breakthrough of the supernatural, then we must win this mind game. We cannot react out of our emotions or logic; we must respond from our spirit. We need to realize that our mindsets can be a stumbling block to the purposes of God. We need to let God show us how we obstruct His will with our wrong thinking and worldly perspectives. So often we start full of faith and vision, and then we lose our sense of purpose and get cynical. When we are first saved, we are ready to pray with everyone for healing—we always believe that God will break through. But as the race of faith continues, we can get disillusioned and lose our passion. We start well, full of good intentions, but then allow our experiences to dictate our destiny. But He is *still* the God of power!

I believe that, whatever the circumstances of your life today, you will see the breakthrough you long for if you do not give up. Ask God to put a fresh tenacity in your heart so that you finish the race, especially if you have underestimated the struggle to the finish line. You will finish your race and cut that tape. God will break out for you. Take courage; He is the God of the breakthrough!

CHAPTER

# Breakthrough
# for Miracles

9

Most of us long to see the power of God break out in the area of
miracles and healing. Many of us have prayed for someone we
know with cancer and then watched them die rather than live.
Our apparent powerlessness to break through, when we know
God has the power to heal, is a constant frustration. I believe
that in these days God wants us to experience a breakout of
signs and wonders in our Western nations like never before. It
is time! I really thank God for the many who *are* healed, but I do
believe it is time to see much more consistency. Here is a
testimony to encourage you:

> In 2005 Rachel was speaking at the Northwest breakthrough
> conference. Afterward she offered to pray for those who had
> physical sickness. The line was long and I saw many who
> seemed to be needier than me, so I hesitated but decided to
> hang back in the line and pray for Rachel. Time was running
> out, and Rachel had to rush off somewhere. But she said to
> those still standing left in the line to make a semicircle and that
> she would quickly go by and lay hands on each of us. She went
> around touching each one on the forehead. . . . When she came
> to me, she put her hand on the right side of my chest and then
> the left.

Little did she know that just the day before I was diagnosed with 85 percent invasive breast cancer. Five weeks later, when I went to be examined, I was completely healed—much to the surprise of the medical world. It was just the quick word of the moment and the slight touch of her fingers, but our God is the greatest in the little moment.

Ruth, Portland, Oregon

Although I have seen God break through with signs and wonders in the West, I still find it much easier to see miracles in the developing nations. While I was in Mysore, India, in May 2006, I went to visit a man called Allen in the hospital after the evening service. The family had pleaded for a "man or woman of God to come and say 'special' prayers"! He was dying from heart disease, his body was in renal collapse and the fluid on his lungs was suffocating him. As we stood and prayed around his bed on this Thursday night, we knew that if God did not heal this man quickly, he would be dead within hours. On Saturday we received a message that he was sitting up in bed eating; on Sunday we heard that he was walking around the hospital; and by the end of the week he was discharged. The whole hospital was amazed, and the doctors knew it was a miracle.

Later in September 2006, one of the pastors went to visit him again and sent this report:

I went and visited Allen and Valerie on Monday evening and was thrilled to see how well he looks. He is walking at least one kilometer per day and has started doing a little work at a school. He will start at another school at the beginning of October. At his last visit to his doctor (a Hindu), the doctor was delighted at his recovery and requested, "Pray a prayer to Jesus for me, too." While I was there I asked him if he'd started playing the guitar again. He had not because he sold his electric one to help with his medical costs. I said I'd have loved to have heard him, so he offered to come around on Tuesday evening to Joel's house and sing ten songs. He duly did, and we had a wonderful time together. I was so moved, especially when he sang "He Touched Me" with so much extra meaning for him.[1]

It was this miracle that provoked me to seek God for answers about the East-versus-West issue of miracles. The research scientist in me began to ask the question, "Why? What is present in India and Africa that makes it easier for us to see the power of God released?" Why did we see Allen virtually raised from his deathbed in Mysore, but then we watch too many friends die of cancer in the West? What are the keys of breakthrough that we are missing? As I began to ask these questions, God began to speak to me about the principles of glory and honor.

## Glory and honor

In places like Africa and India, a culture of honor exists that is sadly absent in the West. We frequently pray, "O God, let Your glory come!" but there is a link between the glory of God and the atmosphere of honor. Where there is honor we will find glory. The Church has pursued glory and forgotten the boundaries of honor. But it is impossible to have the glory of God released unless we first create an atmosphere of honor. The Scriptures show how glory and honor are closely inter-linked. This verse from Revelation is typical: "Thou art worthy, O Lord, *to receive glory and honour and power*: for thou hast created all things, and for thy pleasure they are and were created" (4:11, KJV, emphasis added).

If we want to see the glory of God break out, we need to understand the principle of honor. To find cultures that carry a

1. Report emailed by Duncan Watkinson, Bangalore, India.

strong sense of honor, you have to travel east rather than west! Historically, while Britain was connected to her strong Christian values, the British were known to be people of their word and had integrity. But since she has systematically disconnected herself from her Christian heritage, Britain can no longer be called a nation of honor. I have realized that if we lose the principle of honor from society, we also lose the presence of God's glory.

## The principle of honor

Sociological studies have identified that the factors of "shame" and "honor" are the basis for the pivotal value systems of society. True honor includes the attitudes of esteem, respect, giving regard to, noticing, giving a high place of recognition to, maintaining the good reputation of and considering. Shame, the opposite of honor, is defined as "humiliation, a loss of standing, a loss of position and disregard."

In other words, to dishonor, or shame, someone is to disregard them. Many people in the West carry this sense of shame and dishonor today and walk with their heads bowed. They feel disregarded and ignored. When people fail to notice us and ignore us, it leaves us feeling hurt and valueless, but God created mankind to live in an atmosphere of honor. We were designed for significance and have a need for affirmation in our lives. When we choose to recognize the worth of others and affirm them, God is attracted by this attitude.

Also, as I continued to examine the nations, I realized that Africa and India still have a cultural respect for God Himself and honor Him, whereas in the West we more often hear an arrogant, mocking attitude that challenges His very existence. No wonder, then, that often the heavens seem like brass to us as we seek to press through for our breakthrough. There are five key aspects of honor that we need to restore if we are to see a shift in the spiritual atmosphere of the West:

## 1. Honor God

Critically, we must truly honor God, not just acknowledge Him when it is convenient to us. To "honor" means that we give Him the full respect He is due. It means to give Him His right standing and position; to regard His opinion and His preference as being the most important; to give due attention to Him and what He says; to acknowledge Him in everything. When we are honoring God, we are always asking, "What can I do for You, God?" Phinehas was a man who had had such a revelation about honor, as we read in Numbers 25:10–13:

> The LORD said to Moses, "Phinehas son of Eleazar, the son of Aaron, the priest, has turned my anger away from the Israelites; *for he was as zealous as I am for my honor among them,* so that in my zeal I did not put an end to them. Therefore tell him I am making my covenant of peace with him. He and his descendants will have a covenant of a lasting priesthood, because *he was zealous for the honor of his God and made atonement for the Israelites.*"
>
> emphasis added

Here we read that God says, "I've found a man who understands honor, just like Me." So God gave Phinehas two blessings. First, God gave him a generational blessing, saying, "You will have an everlasting covenant upon your lineage." Why? Because he was passionate about God's honor. Second, God allowed Phinehas to stand in the gap for his nation, to make atonement for the Israelites. At that time the Israelites were under a curse. A plague was afflicting them and many were dying. Because Phinehas honored God, he was positioned

to become a mediator for the nation and break the curse of the plague so that they could be healed. 
      Just as Phinehas experienced blessing because of his attitude of honor, so we find that Eli's sons' *lack* of honor brought a curse on their whole household and their father. We read in 1 Samuel 2:30 that God despises those who despise Him:

> "Therefore the LORD, the God of Israel, declares: 'I promised that your house and your father's house would minister before me forever.' But now the LORD declares: 'Far be it from me! Those who honor me I will honor, but those who despise me will be disdained.' "

If our nations despise God and His ways, then we cannot expect God to show honor toward us. Only to the honorable does God show Himself honorable. I often fear for our Western nations who no longer honor God, as they change their attitude from honoring to despising so the atmosphere over the nation changes from blessings to curses. Thus we live in a place where miracles do not happen readily. We see this principle under-lined further as we read this Scripture in Malachi:

> "If you do not listen, and *if you do not set your heart to honor my name*," says the LORD Almighty, "I will send a curse upon you, *and I will curse your blessings*. Yes, I have already cursed them, because you have not set your heart to honor me."
>
> 2:2, emphasis added

If we do not set our hearts to honor, God says that even our blessings will be cursed. When I examined the root meaning of this phrase *to curse*, I found it means "to withhold." In other words, when we make a decision to set our hearts in an attitude of dishonor, God will withhold even the blessings owed to us!

So if we want to see the breakthrough of miracles in our nations again, we must make a deliberate decision to set our hearts to honor so that we can receive every spiritual blessing God has for us.

We can see that this principle even operated in the life of Jesus. When Jesus returned back to Nazareth, His hometown, He encountered a wall of offense and dishonor. We read in Matthew 13:57–58 the following:

> And they took offense at him. But Jesus said to them, "Only in his hometown and in his own house is a prophet without honor." And he did not do many miracles there because of their lack of faith.

The lack of honor shown to Jesus even limited His miraculous flow so that He did not do many miracles in that place. Dishonor creates a restrictive atmosphere, limits the manifestation of the glory of God and shuts down people's faith. If Jesus Himself was not able to flow in miracles very easily when He was under an atmosphere of disbelief and dishonor, it is no wonder that we struggle, too! If we are going to change this atmosphere in our nations, we need to recognize that honor first needs to be expressed toward God and then shown to others around us.

## 2. Honor gender

Across the nations there is a move to blur gender boundaries. "Homosexual, heterosexual, lesbian—you choose, it doesn't really matter" is the message society is promoting in the name of "tolerance." Society and the media say, "Let's go unisex. What's the big deal? We can experiment!" But the Bible says, "No—there are boundaries." There is male. There is female. God designed us to relate as men and women, husband and wife, masculine and feminine. We were created separate beings but made to come together to discover the whole. We need to honor the design of God even if our culture rejects God's ways.

The gender battle began back in the 1960s when women who had been severely crushed rebelled. They were determined to show that they were as capable as men. In the process of their struggle for freedom, however, they damaged many men. These days, if a man sees a woman struggling with a heavy item and offers to help, he often gets the terse response, "I can manage!" Or if you open the door for a lady, she lets it bang in your face! Unfortunately, as men have tried to honor women, women have given dishonor in return.

But men have dominated and crushed women for years. All false religions and cults crush and demean women. Islam, Hinduism, religious cults and, dare I say, even "religious" Christian churches have rules and regulations designed to suppress women. Most of us have encountered this attitude at one time: "Shut up, woman! Your opinion isn't important," or words to that effect. So women have either been really broken and abused or reacted by becoming very dominant and strong. But we in the Church must find the right way in which we can honor the distinctions between male and female. We must honor the creation of God and work practically to honor one another, especially in our marriages.

First Peter 3:7 says, "Husbands, in the same way be considerate as you live with your wives, and treat them with respect as the weaker partner and as heirs with you of the gracious gift of life, *so that nothing will hinder your prayers*" (emphasis added).

Many women react to this verse and feel that it shows that the Bible is sexist. But I want to point out that this word "weaker" does not mean "lesser," nor does it mean "inferior," which many read into it. What it does mean is this: of lesser capacity either physically and/or emotionally. What the Bible is actually saying is, "Come on, husbands. When your wife is under emotional or physical pressure, your job is to protect and help her. Do not make her feel like a nuisance, but take the load and encourage her." As we do this we see that the Bible promises us that "nothing will hinder our prayers." So if we want to see a breakthrough in our prayer for miracles, we need to learn how to honor one another!

### 3. Honor age

All through Scripture we see that the Bible honors the older rather than the younger. God honors age and gray hair. Again, our culture has turned away from these biblical values. We have created a culture where people are terrified of looking old, and society believes that youth is better. But the Bible says, "I will honor you with long life." It is an honor to be given the gift of age! We need to honor those who are older among us. We need to give them value; we must make sure they feel valued.

The Bible also speaks about honoring our parents. In the book of Exodus, that is one of God's top ten rules for life. The word used for honor is *kabod*, which is the same word that is used elsewhere to describe the residential glory of God. Then in 1 Timothy chapter 5, Paul talks to Timothy frankly about how to relate to people of different ages in his congregation, saying, "Timothy, you are a young man with a lot of responsibility, but make sure you always speak to the older men in the right way. Treat your widows and older women with respect. Keep a right attitude to the young people, too. Teach the older men to work with the younger men and make sure the young people do not dishonor them. Just because you are a young leader and younger people will be attracted to your leadership, don't forget to keep an atmosphere of honor toward the older people in the house of God" (my paraphrase).

You can hear Paul's exhortation to honor. In 1 Timothy 5:8 Paul says, "And remember, Timothy, just because you are in the ministry does not mean you can neglect your family. If you don't take care of your own flesh and blood, then you have dishonored all the work you are doing, and you are worse than an unbeliever!" (my paraphrase). So we need to note that if we want God to bless our ministry, we must first bless our family—especially as they get older—or the resulting atmosphere of dishonor over our lives will limit the flow of the miraculous through us.

### 4. Honor your word

It used to be said, "A gentleman's word is his bond." This saying is rooted in our Christian heritage. We know God by His Word, and His Word is sacrosanct—and we are called to be imitators of God. Once again our culture has turned its back on this principle. We tend to give our word to someone and then, if that promise becomes inconvenient, we retract it and give some excuse. Today we see a constantly increasing amount of legislation, the aim of which is basically to make sure people keep their word! Whatever the situation, people have a habit of breaking their word. It might be in business: A deal is agreed upon, and then a day later someone comes in with a better offer, so we go back to the first person and say, "Sorry, I've changed my mind." I believe God is challenging the Church to behave in a different way. We must keep our word, even if it hurts. God is exhorting us, "Come on, Church! Your word must have integrity." That is God-culture, Kingdom-culture.

This area is vitally important for us as parents. We need to model the principles of honor to our children by being people of our word. My son, David, was born in Kenya while we were missionaries there. When he was fourteen he really wanted to visit Kenya, and so he began to ask me regularly if he could go until I promised, "Okay, the next time I go to Kenya I will take you with me." Almost immediately I got an invitation to go to Kenya. Then I thought, *Oh no, how am I going to take David with me? Never mind, it wasn't that serious.* But then I checked myself. *Hang on, Rachel! Just because it's not very convenient, I can't dismiss it like that!* So I went to David and said, "I've just been invited to Kenya. I promised I would take you. I don't know how it's going to work, to be perfectly honest, but if you want to come with me, we'll have to pray and ask God to make a way." David had a look at the dates and came back to me, saying that actually he felt he should not go this time because it clashed with certain events at school. He released me from my promise. It is so important that we keep our word to our kids and do not just disregard our promises to them.

To finish the story, I then said to David that we should pray and ask God to open up another opportunity for him to go. Three days later my parents came to visit us from America. My mom took me to one side and said, "I felt God challenge me on the plane to take David to Kenya. What do you think about that?" I said, "I think it's perfect!" She was going in August, which was the perfect time for David—no school, no complications. She asked to talk to David about it, and afterwards he came out of the room, beaming. "I'm going to Kenya!" He had an amazing time, and God really blessed him.

If we want God to fulfill every promise to us and see the breakthrough, we must keep our word and be honorable.

### 5. Honor authority

If we want to have spiritual authority and see signs and wonders released, then we must also honor authority. Romans 12:10 says, "Be devoted to one another in brotherly love. Honor one another above yourselves." Having an attitude of honor toward one another, especially those in spiritual authority, is a safe place to be. If you respect authority, then God can trust you with His power.

"But you haven't met my leaders!" some will protest. True, but even so, you can choose not to deliberately dishonor them in front of others, even if you do not agree with everything they do and say. Some may also ask, "How do we honor ungodly leaders?" (i.e., political leaders who do not know Christ). Maybe you watch what is happening in government and are furious at some of the legislation that is passed, which runs contrary to godly principles. "How can I honor that?" you ask. The biblical principle is that we honor the position of the person even if we cannot honor his or her actions. As we make a decision to give honor to the position, God then holds that person accountable for his or her actions.

When we take these principles of honor seriously, we set the atmosphere for the miraculous to break through. Honor creates a breakthrough atmosphere! Many times it will cost you to do the right thing, and you will have to make a choice to honor your parents, boss, youth leader, pastor, spouse and so on. You can decide to honor your father's position even when he has not been a great dad, even if you come from a dysfunctional family. You can honor your husband's position before God even if he is not really caring and not fulfilling his role properly. If you do that, God will take care of the rest.

The Bible is very specific about how we honor our spiritual leaders. Often in the Church we have become hesitant about really honoring our leaders because we are afraid that they will abuse their power. In the process we have lost the outpouring of signs and wonders in our nations. Here we have the choice and the privilege to give honor, and in this case double honor. First Timothy 5:17 says, "The elders who direct the affairs of the church well *are worthy of double honor, especially those whose work is preaching and teaching*" (emphasis added).

Why are those who preach and teach worthy of double honor? Let's go back to the definition of honor. Honor gives position, it lifts up, it releases authority and it gives regard, standing and position. When you come to teach and preach, there is a double responsibility. The Bible also says that signs and wonders will follow the preaching of the Word. But you need the atmosphere of honor to lift you into a position of breakthrough. If the Word is preached and goes forth in an atmosphere of great honor, then the way is prepared for the glory to come down. It is amazing how you feel a greater anointing is released when you teach and preach in a place where you know that the people honor you! This atmosphere pulls something more out of you than you could normally give. If you give double honor, then you will receive a double reward. You will see double the miracles, double the blessing, double the breakthrough. Let us pick up this key of honor and use it and watch the mighty doors of miracles open across the nations!

# Breakthrough in Finances

## 10

## Outrageous generosity

I discovered a long time ago that Jesus is the most generous person I have ever known. When you really get to know Him, you will fall in love with His spirit of outrageous generosity. There is nothing like the goodness and overwhelming generosity of God to make you feel so cherished and grateful for His attention and kindness in your life. When I least deserve a gift, He just blesses me, and when I feel I am worthless, He gives me such value. Wow! What a God!

Once, when I was visiting Seattle, a lovely woman came and sat next to me and said, "Rachel, I want to bless you with my spiritual gift and take you shopping." She insisted on taking me to the best shopping mall in the area and to one of the most expensive stores. I knew it was frightfully expensive, because it was one of those places where nothing has a price tag on it! She then said to me, "I want to select a few things that I want to buy for you, and then I want you to choose which one you like the most and let me give it to you as a blessing." She ended up buying me an entire outfit—shoes, a jacket, a skirt and pants. Then on top of that she said, "Okay, now we need to get the makeup!" This lady just spoiled me from top to bottom. At first I felt uncomfortable by this generosity, but once I relaxed and decided to receive, I left the mall feeling like a queen, because that's what generosity can do for you. And just as it can do that in the natural, so it can in the spiritual. You feel like a prince or a princess when you have truly encountered the generosity of God toward you. You feel so undeserving and yet so humbled and honored that God would bless you.

So often in the Church we understand the principle of spiritual generosity, yet we miss out on the practical aspects of it. We need to be channels that actively release "material" generosity toward each other. We can earnestly pray for a financial breakthrough in many situations, but often people do not need more prayer; they need an offering! Recently I was ministering in a church in Scotland. During the notices, one of the young people stood up and shared a vision to attend a youth camp in Sweden, asking the church to pray for the financial supply for the youth to go. As they shared their vision, I was stirred in my heart. These kids wanted to go and get trained so they could work in evangelism. This was no holiday adventure but a deep call and a missions trip. After requesting prayer for their financial breakthrough, I was invited to come and preach. I was still stirred by their vision, and so instead of speaking I took up an offering. I challenged the church to give to their own youth. In this one offering we were able to give these kids the answer to their prayers, and there were many tears as we watched them be blessed, and their faith was rewarded! The world around us does not understand the language of spiritual generosity very well when it is preached in isolation—it needs to see something physically expressed. We need to give our time to the lonely and food to the hungry, and we need to demonstrate God's generosity by being His hands toward them—just as the lady from Seattle was His kindness to me.

When it comes to giving, we can often give the right appearance on the outside and say all the right things, but on the inside we have other agendas. We are not truly generous and our motives are tainted. We give because we feel guilty; we give because we feel obliged; but we should give out of the overflow of generosity, which cries out, "I must bless you!" God wants us to become outrageously generous and learn the breakthrough of giving with great joy, free from fear!

People who know me know that, although I live in the United Kingdom and have a British passport, I am not very English in my outlook. I sound as though I am and I look as though I am, but my first sixteen years were spent growing up in India. I am a missionary kid. As a result, much of my cultural mentality has been influenced by Third World attitudes. I returned briefly to the United Kingdom to complete my university studies in London, got married to Gordon and then left for Africa, where we lived as missionaries for nearly six years. It was while we were in Africa that God taught me how to minister. I grew up in my marriage and with my kids in Africa. I did not live in England for any length of time until I was thirty years old.

When I finally moved back to the United Kingdom permanently, one of the things that shocked me—and I do not mean to offend anyone by this—was how cautious people were to share any of their possessions! When we left England, we sold our house and our car and gave away nearly everything we had. It had been our joy to bless many people in our church with various items. But when we came home, we found people very reluctant to lend *us* the things that we needed while we tried to reestablish ourselves. We had lived in Africa as missionaries and become so used to a generous and liberal mentality, where people gave to each other and loaned items all the time, that this new attitude was alien to us! We had lived life by routinely giving money and things away, even when we had very little ourselves. This new atmosphere was a challenge. Nevertheless, God began to challenge us and said, *Do not get* bitter, *but live life demonstrating a* better *way. Make a decision to live life with an opposite spirit.* It is so easy to react to a stingy atmosphere by withholding yourself, but no, we must act in the opposite spirit and give!

During this time I made this Scripture one of the mottos of my life, and I have tried to live with this attitude since: "A generous [wo]man will prosper; [s]he who refreshes others will ... be refreshed" (Proverbs 11:25).

We need to rediscover our heart of kindness in the Church. There is a generous heart in the West, which is often seen during times of disaster and international crisis, but God is beginning to provoke us to be generous in our everyday lives. I believe that God wants His people, corporately, to be filled with an outrageous generosity. But there are strongholds that hold back this attitude of generosity. What are they, and how can we break through to see a release of finance for the Kingdom of God?

## The stronghold of materialism

An attitude of generosity and liberal giving is not a natural characteristic of mankind. Most of us find ourselves more selfish than generous if we are honest. But in Western society, people struggle even more as they live under a stronghold of greed and materialism. This atmosphere influences the way in which we think and react, just as Indian and African culture influenced me when I lived there. In India and Africa, there is a real sacrificial generosity shown toward others. If you are the guest of a family, they will literally kill the last chicken they own to feed you. They thrive on a spirit of generosity.

In the West, however, despite our vast wealth, a spirit of poverty reigns. In fact, we are so accustomed to it that we scarcely realize we are living under it. We do not notice that we tend to withhold rather than give. For this reason, we need to ask the Holy Spirit to search our lives and ask God, "Have I become stingy?" I believe God is calling the Church to break out against the tide of greed, materialism and self-obsession to demonstrate an "unreasonable" generosity.

I believe that one of the keys to seeing an opening of the heavens and an outpouring of signs and wonders in the West is a proper understanding of how to handle our money before God. Nearly every revival that has taken place has been characterized by a change in the attitudes of the people of God toward money, resulting in a release of an outrageous, generous spirit.

John Wesley once said, "When I have money, I get rid of it quickly, lest it find a way into my heart." To change our mindset toward our finances does take effort and time. Why? Because we have all been influenced by the fear of financial ruin and the lack of money. But I believe God wants to break us out of this mindset.

I knew a wonderful Zulu pastor who used to teach on the spirit of generosity. In meetings he would sometimes say to the congregation, "How many of you want to give a generous offering to the Lord?" The people would put their hands up. Then he would say, "Take out your wallets. I will teach you how to give generously to the Lord." They would take their wallets out, and then he would say, "Now give your wallet to the person on your left, and give generously to the Lord!" The idea of such a thing probably terrifies most of us! But if we look back at the early Church when the Holy Spirit was first poured out, we notice that this outpouring changed people's attitudes toward their possessions. Acts 2:44–45 says, "All the believers were together and had everything in common. Selling their possessions and goods, they gave to anyone as he had need." And Acts 4:33 says, "With great power the apostles continued to testify to the resurrection of the Lord Jesus, and much grace was upon them all."

That phrase "much grace" is important. It was "much grace" that changed people's hearts and caused them to act in a different way. Previously, people had been selfish and inward looking, but now there were no needy people among the community of believers. From time to time, those who owned land or houses sold them and brought the money from the sale and put it at the apostles' feet. This money was then distributed to anyone as he or she had need. Can you imagine that happening at your church? This verse in Acts is quite a challenge, isn't it? People sold all their land and inheritance, and what did they do? Go down to the bank and transfer it into their pension plan? No! They put it at the apostles' feet and trusted them to have the wisdom from God to make a wise investment into people's lives. It is so different to our way of thinking—the equivalent of us taking our inheritance money and giving it all to the church leadership team, trusting them to distribute it according to the needs of each member of the congregation. This is radical!

I am not saying this is what we all need to do, before you get alarmed and set fire to this book! I am just trying to be a little bit provocative. I find it fascinating that whenever we begin to discuss the practical day-to-day issues of money, people withdraw and become defensive and protective. As the boundaries of our comfort zones and personal space are challenged by these suggestions, we respond with, "Now you are going too far!" We react and then tend to hold on to our wallets very tightly.

But I do not want to be controlled by power of money or the

fear of having none! I want the Holy Spirit to be so in control of me that I am gripped by a spirit of generosity, not greed. God once said this to me: *Rachel, give Me access to your bank account and I'll give you access to* Mine. Is this a fair deal? Absolutely! But we are so reluctant to trust Him and do it.

When I was first married, I was terrified of giving generously. I was "Mrs. Squirrel," who saved everything and made sure that life was safe financially. I could not see the God of "more than enough." I was controlled by an "apple pie" mentality that said, "If I give this away, then there is less pie left for me. How do I know if I will have enough?" I could not see the river of provision that flows from God. God's economy works on an entirely different basis. As we give to Him, He flows even more back to us. His river never gets depleted or runs dry—there is an endless supply. We need to learn to trust and break through our fears and to give and receive!

## The stronghold of idolatry

Idolatry—the worship, respect or awe given to false gods—is one of the things that consistently shuts up the heavens and prevents personal breakthrough. All through Scripture God states that He hates this sin. Money has become a god in our society, and many of us do not even realize that we bow down to its power. How can we know if money has become a god in our life? We just have to examine what controls our decisions and obedience. We all know that we should love and serve God. We should let Him govern our lives. We should live in reverential fear of Him and respect Him. We all agree with these statements. But if we allow money to rule us and have a voice in our lives, then our response toward God will be compromised. Matthew 6:24 says, "No one can serve two masters. Either he will hate the one and love the other, or he will be devoted to the one and despise the other. You cannot serve both God and Money."

If money has become too strong an influence in your life, you will notice that your world seems to revolve around it. Your mind will constantly come back to your financial situation. If, when you wake up in the morning, the first thing you worry about is money—*When will my salary check clear? I must remember to pay that bill...*—then money is probably ruling your life. If you fear bankruptcy or everything in your life is planned around money, then money is becoming your master. It is so easy to fall into this trap. In our society, "managing our money" is so ingrained into the national psyche that thinking about money all the time is portrayed as being a responsible thing. I do believe that God wants us to be good stewards of our money, as it is His money and we should use it wisely—but it must not become an obsession!

My husband, Gordon, had a very different attitude toward money than I did when we first got married. Whereas I was "Mrs. Squirrel," he was "Mr. Give-it-away-quick." Gordon really struggled with having any money, as he always felt guilty and so just gave it away anywhere. God had to teach him to steward his money. He had to realize that money was not dirty but an important asset for the Kingdom, and he needed to give it with care.

God then began to challenge this "Mrs. Squirrel" attitude in my life: *Rachel, you have more trust in your money than in Me as your provider. You trust your bank account and your life insurance policy to take care of you more than you trust Me as your Father to provide for you.*

God went on to say to me, *Many of you find it hard to serve Me but find it easy to serve money.* I objected to this initially, but then He said, *Rachel, you will work if you're paid!* It is true. You feel a sense of reward when you're paid. Men in particular draw a great deal of self-worth from earning their salary. That's why redundancy affects them so deeply. They feel robbed of their status. Unwittingly, money has come to represent position and power to people, and their identity as children under God's care has diminished accordingly. We no longer rely on God but on our ability to earn.

## The love of money

We need to understand that money is one of the most useful and spiritual commodities there is and is not wrong in itself, but if we are not careful it can become a snare. We must decide who will be the master. Money is a wonderful servant but a terrible master! First Timothy 6:10 says, "For the love of money is a root of all kinds of evil. Some people, eager for money, have wandered from the faith and pierced themselves with many griefs."

The love of money is a root for all kinds of evil, because once you start to love the power of money and it captivates your heart, it leads you into every type of sin. Money now becomes the voice that directs you. This then shuts down your spiritual life, and suddenly heaven is closed.

Hebrews 13:5–6 reaffirms,

> Keep your lives free from the love of money and be content with what you have, because God has said, "Never will I leave you; never will I forsake you." So we say with confidence, "The Lord is my helper; I will not be afraid. What can man do to me?"

This was such a revelation to me. God has promised us that where money is concerned, He's never going to leave us destitute. He will not abandon us. You can say with the utmost confidence, "God is my helper. He pays my paycheck! I don't need to be afraid because I don't have any money. What can man do to me? I've got God. He'll never leave me, never desert me!" Often we use this Scripture in other contexts, but here we can clearly see that this promise is connected to our finances. God has said do not worry about your money because He will never leave you!

I was 24 when Gordon and I sold our business and our home and left everything to go to Africa, and I have not lived on a designated salary since. While we lived in Africa, any gifts in Sterling were converted into Kenyan shillings and were a real blessing! The money went a long way. But now I live in England and it is a bit different. We have been through some tough times. There are times when you work hard but are rewarded with little. Some people think that since I am a woman ministering to others, my husband will pay the bills and so I do not need an honorarium. Other times I have been given a pot of homemade jam or a bunch of flowers as a ministry gift after a weekend's work!

Consequently, there have been times when I returned from a ministry trip and struggled. I thought, *Lord, I've driven for hours; I've worked my guts out.* The people shook my hand on their way out and said, "Rachel, we've been so blessed; we've been so overwhelmed," yet they gave me a pot of jam and a bunch of flowers. Sometimes the host of the meeting would even tell me, "We've had fantastic offerings; people have been so generous, and something's happened!" Yet I had not seen a financial breakthrough in my life!

On one occasion I was driving back down the freeway, having given my all, knowing that when I got home there would be two teenage children to look after, and we were struggling financially at the time. I was questioning God about this and He said to me, *Who do you trust to pay you—other people or Me?* Instantly, I said, "God, I want to trust You to pay me. Please help me!"

This was the beginning of a three-year battle that eventually led to a great breakthrough. The first thing God taught me was to be a source and resource to others. I wanted to receive a financial breakthrough, but first I had to be generous to others. We were obedient to this, but initially our situation seemed to get worse, not better. The more I learned to be obedient and give, the more people were convinced that we had private money and did not need any help! So we gave literally in raw obedience again and again, believing that there would be a harvest and a breakthrough in time.

During this season, the pastor of one church I ministered to said publicly to the congregation, "Tonight, we are going to give the entire offering to Rachel—this will be a gift to bless her." At the end of the meeting, the church treasurer came up to me very excited (the pastor did not know this) and said, "We've never taken such a big offering! It's £1,600. I am so thrilled because you've so blessed our church." Later, I opened the envelope they had given me and discovered a check for £200. Shocked, I thought, *What's going on, God?* I eventually felt that I should call the pastor, so I did. I said, "Look, the treasurer came to me and said this . . ." I told him the whole story. The pastor replied, and I quote, "It's God's responsibility to keep you humble and our responsibility to keep you poor!"

As he said these words, I realized the enormous battle we have to break through into a Kingdom mentality with our finances. The anger I had felt melted, and I found myself praying for the Church to get a revelation of the God of generosity. I believe it is essential that the Church becomes gripped with a passion to see finances released for the next season. We must become generous givers! We have been sold a lie by the enemy that says if we let go of our money we're going to end up poor and broke. It is not true! For a decade Gordon and I lived in the United Kingdom with no promised salary whatsoever, and we were amazingly, abundantly blessed. There have been times when our faith has been stretched to the limit, but God always pays us on time! You can trust God. He has the ability to pay all your bills if only you will entrust Him with everything.

## The money seed

Money is powerful seed. We have to learn to sow and harvest this seed for the Kingdom of God. Money is dynamite; it has power. In the right hands money can be used for good, but equally, in the wrong hands it can bring destruction. We see the effects of the abuse of money on the pages of our tabloid newspapers every day.

Before our money can be used to produce fruit in the Kingdom of God, it has to be planted into the "soil" of the Kingdom. It must be sown with faith into a field of ministry, not just carelessly thrown in the offering basket. If you invest your money into a particular field in the Kingdom and water it with prayer and faith, a harvest will grow in that particular area of the Kingdom. If you want to eat mangoes, then you plant mango trees! In the same way, if you want to see a dynamic children's ministry grow, then you must invest your money into people or places with a good children's work. If you want to see prayer touch cities, then invest your money into the lives of people who pray and lead prayer ministries. The field into which you plant your seed is important, as it will affect the harvest that comes forth.

Numerous people who live with this mentality have testified to the way in which God has amazingly multiplied their seed. But the harvest does not return to us in order to increase our standard of living or help us live more comfortably.

Rather, God multiplies it so that we can increase our level of generosity toward others. Maybe your recent pay increase was not seed for you to "eat" in your life but Kingdom seed for you to give away. Paul wrote about this in 2 Corinthians chapter 9:

> Each man should give what he has decided in his heart to give, not reluctantly or under compulsion, for God loves a cheerful giver. And God is able to make all grace abound to you, so that in all things at all times, having all that you need, you will abound in every good work. As it is written: "He has scattered abroad his gifts to the poor; his righteousness endures forever." Now he who supplies seed to the sower and bread for food will also supply *and increase your store of seed* and will enlarge the harvest of your righteousness. You will be made rich in every way so that you can be generous on every occasion, and through us your generosity will result in thanksgiving to God. This service that you perform is not only supplying the needs of God's people but is also overflowing in many expressions of thanks to God.
>
> verses 7–12, emphasis added

We need to understand the biblical principle of sowing and reaping. There are times when you need to take your money and sow for a specific harvest. You need to sow in line with the destiny and the calling of God upon your life. God has put a burden on my heart for cities, especially the city of London, so I look for fertile ground in London where I can invest into the Kingdom. I also have a heart for young people who need training and love to sponsor them in Bible school so that they can develop their destiny call. What are your passions? Is it youth work, orphanages, evangelism projects, translation work or a particular nation or city? Start to invest into this "soil" and watch your investment grow and multiply.

## Tithes and offerings

The verse of Malachi 3:10 is a familiar one that talks about bringing our tithe to God:

> "Bring the whole tithe into the storehouse, that there may be food in my house. Test me in this," says the LORD Almighty, "and see if I will not throw open the floodgates of heaven and pour out so much blessing that you will not have room enough for it."

When I read about "floodgates," I visualize the gates of a lock on an English canal. The gates are there to hold in a body of water that is on a different, higher level than the rest of the canal. When you give your tithe to God, you unlock the floodgates. The sluice gates of heaven open, and down flows blessing that touches every area of your life. This blessing includes the release of financial favor, but so much more. Your body, soul, mind and spirit all prosper. God blesses all that you have, including your generational line!

I know people who are generous givers and can see the tangible effect it has on their lives. They are usually the happiest people—they have an inner joy. When Gordon and I pastored our church, I could tell, without speaking to the church treasurer, who the real givers in the church were. It was written on their faces! Their lives and money were given to God and they were blessed. I am not saying that they were protected from all difficulty, but they carried an extraordinary grace even in the tough times.

Some people argue that tithing only applies to the Old Testament era, being part of a legalistic system of control that is no longer applicable now that we are living under grace. I really prayed about this for a long time and asked the Lord, "God, show me what is right and wrong." This is what He said to me: *Under the law you keep a rule and a regulation. It is a simple action performed from your mind, a decision that you logically make.* That is the process by which we keep the law. In the Bible the law says, "Do not commit adultery," and so if you do not get into bed with anyone else's partner and have sex, technically you have kept the letter of the law, even if you have committed adultery with your imagination in your heart and mind. The law, therefore, only controls and judges *actions*, not *intentions*.

Under grace it is different. Grace is the favor of God given to those who love Him. Here God tests the attitudes and motivations of the heart. Here our decision is connected by faith to what we believe with our spirit, rather than pure logic. Grace operates through the spiritual link to your mind and body. Grace depends on relationship, not just rules. We do not just want to give an appearance of right; we want to bring pleasure to God by presenting right actions with right motivations. This gift of grace challenges us to keep our hearts right before God, and consequently our actions remain within the constraints of the law.

Under grace, "Do not commit adultery" means "Do not even look at a woman lustfully," as Jesus explained. Our heart attitude has to be correct. Grace goes much further than mere actions; grace always outdoes the law. I believe the same is true regarding tithes and offerings. The law says 10 percent of all we have belongs to God, but real grace will want to go beyond 10 percent! The law says, "Give me 10 percent," but grace says, "God, I want to bless You; I want to give You everything. God, let me be like You!" The attitude of grace is not, "What is the minimum I have to give?" because there are no rules. The attitude of grace says, "What is the most I can give, as I want to bless God?" Living under grace does not give us an excuse to get away with not giving to God. His grace should enable us to take greater risks and to give more financially. Ten percent should be our minimum and 100 percent our aim!

## Our attitude toward missions

As we look at this subject of financial breakthrough, I would also like to examine our attitudes toward financially supporting missions projects, both at home in our communities and in other nations. I have noticed that the people of the Western Church can be incredibly generous when it comes to supporting missionaries if they work in developing nations, but they are reluctant to invest in what is happening on their doorstep. Recently, a wonderful Chinese missionary came to visit our church, and over a period of five days we raised £30,000 to support his work. I was thrilled by this gift and believe that we should bless these nations. But I began to realize that we have a blind spot. We have many self-sacrificing missionaries working on the streets of our own cities in God-ordained ministries, and numbers of them are struggling through lack of financial support. We will give generously to the poor across the sea, but we find it hard to give to the needy across the street.

If we want to see the atmosphere of spiritual poverty broken in our own nations, then we need to ensure that money for the work of God is given to our communities. We need to invest righteous seed into the streets of our communities to support Kingdom projects. If we always export our seed elsewhere, then we will never reap a harvest in our own land. We can overlook the poor and needy that we see every day and abandon them, sending our money to the unknown of Africa. I believe we should invest in other nations and give generously to the poor, but I also believe we need to recognize and add the harvest fields of our own cities to our target zone!

When Jesus commissioned His disciples to take the Gospel far and wide, He said, "But you *will* receive power when the Holy Spirit comes on you; and you *will* be my *witnesses* in Jerusalem, and in all Judea and Samaria, and to the ends of the earth" (Acts 1:8, emphasis added).

We are called to be witnesses at home first, then regionally, and finally globally. In the Western Church, we have tended to care for the needs of the nations and forget the suffering on our doorstep. We begin globally, and the immediate needs around us go unanswered. We should ask God where we need to see financial breakthrough and then begin to invest our seed. Jesus was the righteous seed of heaven sown into the unrighteous ground of this world so that He could bring a righteous harvest of sons and daughters into heaven. Let us do the same and sow seed for a Kingdom purpose at home and away!

## Your gift is more than money

Pouring resources into God's Kingdom is more than an offering; it is an act of spiritual warfare. Maybe you have never thought of giving in those terms before. It is an act of war because every time we give in faith, we are coming in the opposite spirit to the spirit of this age, and we challenge the strongholds of greed and materialism. This spirit of generosity unlocks the heavens and opens a path for breakthrough in our lives. Obedient sacrifice opens heavenly blessings. Jesus died and gave His life, and we are still living in His breakthrough.

Our gift is much more than the money we give; it represents a giving of our very life. Take a fifty-dollar bill in your hand. Now work out how long it took you to earn that money. However long it took you to earn it represents a portion of your life—your time and effort invested in that bill. This is why, when we give our money back to the Lord, it is symbolic of us rededicating our lives to Him. It is part of our worship to God. We are surrendering another part of our life to Him. Every time we do this, it touches the heart of God. God gave us His Son, a part of Himself, and now we should generously give back our wealth and lives to Him.

## Provision and vision working together

If we are going to see the breakthrough we desire, then we are going to have to learn how to wisely partner our money with the visions and dreams of God. So often good visions do not have the financial backing they need to build them. Therefore, we need Kingdom partnerships of vision and provision to be born.

In Luke's gospel we catch a glimpse of such a partnership. In Luke 5:4 Jesus challenged Peter to launch out into the deep and let down his nets for a catch. In this Scripture Peter represents the "dreamer" or "visionary," and Jesus challenged him to get out of his comfort zone and stretch into a new area of ministry, asking Peter to trust that Jesus would provide all his needs and more. Many times the Holy Spirit comes to us and moves us into new areas of ministry. Maybe we start a feeding program for the poor or begin a ministry for abused mothers, and we launch out into the deep on His word. The "boat" of vision always has to move out first. Then we read,

> When they had done so, they caught such a large number of fish that their nets began to break. *So they signaled their partners in the other boat to come and help them,* and they came and filled both boats so full that they began to sink. . . . So they pulled their boats up on shore, left everything and followed him.
>
> Luke 5:6–7, 11, emphasis added

You will often find that as soon as a vision is launched on a word from God, the people with the vision discover they cannot tackle the project alone. The size of the provision needed to support the vision seems overwhelming. At this point, many of us begin to act like spectators and say things like, "I knew it was a crazy idea. He could never pull off such a big project here." But when Peter began to have that sinking feeling, he was not independent—he called to his partners. I believe that visionaries need to develop relationships so that they can signal to their partners for help and advice. We need friends who can advise us with business strategy, give us money, help us with building plans and in many other areas give support and practical help. Too often the boat of vision goes out alone without these relationships to come alongside, and so the boat sinks. Even when these two boats were working together, they still nearly sank, but two was better than one, and they survived!

In Luke's account, finally we read that both boats were totally filled and came back to shore. It was mission accomplished *together*; they had fulfilled the task, seen a mighty harvest and been able to bring it in without disaster. I believe that if we are going to see more God-inspired projects reach completion, then we must see more partnerships of vision and provision working together for the Kingdom of God.

This is the day for financial breakthrough in our lives. Now is the day to see His Kingdom come on earth just as it is in heaven. We need to see the signs, wonders and miracles break through. We need to see finances released so that we can see our cities turned upside down for God. It is time to see Jesus back on our streets.

# Breakthrough in Cities

## Seeing the "Jesus factor" back on the streets

Today most of us feel the tension between the sacred and the secular, our church life and our everyday working environment. Although we know we should be carriers of light and take the Kingdom principles of God into our communities, we find it hard to see how our value systems will have the power to penetrate the thick layers of cynicism around us. The walls of opposition seem to have become so strong that our Christian values appear trivial to most and irrelevant to the rest. So begins the struggle between what we know the Word of God says about our authority over our geography as believers, and the reality of our apparent powerlessness that we experience in everyday life. Whether it is privately in the place of prayer at home or while walking the corridors at our place of work, we all want our faith to have a real, external expression that carries an authority. We know what the Bible says, and we know what should be happening as we represent Christ where we are. We want to pray for the sick and those in distress and see quick results. We know that according to the biblical standard we should be seeing signs and wonders; laying hands on the sick and seeing them recover; seeing demons cast out and even the dead raised. And yet, somehow it just never seems to happen like we know it should. We need to see a real expression of Jesus back on the streets of our cities.

Many in the Western Church today are experiencing a great weariness and frustration with their own impotency. We know full well that our experience of life does not match up to the Word of God. We desperately want the same power and authority that the early apostles had, so that we can do what God made us to do. In fact, we want to do what we know we are *called* to do.

Sometimes I sense the intimidation that the sons of Sceva must have felt in Acts 19:15 when they tried to deliver a demon-possessed man. The evil spirit they were trying to cast out challenged them and said, "Jesus I know, and I know about Paul, but *who are you?*" (emphasis added). Do you ever feel that confrontation of the enemy threatening your dignity? Do you have confidence that the enemy knows who you are? I know that whenever I feel this challenge, it triggers a cry within me, and I want to know that the devil has to acknowledge that he knows who I am. I want the enemy to be fearful of me and my life. When I get up in the morning, I want the demons of hell to tremble when they feel the floor move and exclaim, "Oh no, she's up! Now we have trouble!" I know that I should consistently carry this authority as a believer, and yet I am yearning for a greater breakthrough so that not only do I know I have this authority, but I know that the devil knows it, too. I want to be in the place where I see my authority in Christ begin to take dominion over where I live and what I am called to possess.

And therein lies our challenge. I believe that the Church is in a struggle of faith to reposition herself correctly in society so that she can reestablish her influence. The challenge for prophetic people everywhere is the need to help the Church find her lost keys of authority and position her to stand again. Ever since the fall in the Garden of Eden, this has been the story of man's struggle: the battle to regain the authority that was pickpocketed by the devil. Satan, in the form of a serpent, came into the Garden and seductively deceived woman and stole man's God-given authority and dominion. Man had been given the authority to rule on earth, but Satan challenged that authority and was successful in stealing it, becoming the prince of the earth. Now we have to challenge that usurped authority and take it back.

## The authority of Jesus

As we look at Jesus, we see a perfect model of using our Kingdom authority. After Jesus was baptized, He entered the wilderness and battled for His destiny. He emerged carrying a new mantle of power and authority—an ability to break through and to see God's Kingdom come. At the beginning of Luke 4 we read, "Jesus, full of the Holy Spirit, returned from the Jordan and was led by the Spirit in the desert" (verse 1).

Up until the time of His baptism, Jesus had a hidden supernatural life. He seemed like an ordinary child. He lived a good life, a sinless life, a life dedicated to God, but as yet His life was not characterized by the *power* of the Holy Spirit. When He had been baptized and the Holy Spirit had come upon Him, however, it was a turning point. Until then He had not revealed anything of the *supernatural* aspect of His life. No great miracles had been recorded during his childhood; nothing extraordinary had been done.

But once he had been baptized, and after His battle with Satan in the wilderness, we start to see a new power working through His life. His "ordinary" had been clothed with the "extraordinary"—the supernatural was now working with the natural! Something had happened in the wilderness, and Jesus now moved in a new level of public authority. He had been led into the wilderness by the Holy Spirit, but He left the wilderness clothed with the power of the Spirit, and He challenged the dark powers in the spiritual realm that ruled the earth, speaking with a new supernatural authority from God.

How had the devil tempted Jesus? What was the challenge of the wilderness? The devil had challenged the very calling on His life, and Jesus had to fight to establish the authority of the destiny on His life. Just a few verses earlier, in Luke 3:21–22, we read,

> When all the people were being baptized, Jesus was baptized too. And as he was praying, heaven was opened and the Holy Spirit descended on him in bodily form like a dove. And a voice came from heaven: *"You are my Son, whom I love;* with you I am well pleased."
>
> emphasis added

Here Jesus is publicly endorsed as the Son of God. The heavens open, and His Father speaks of the destiny of Jesus over His life. This must have been one of the deepest spiritual moments for Jesus, hearing the sound of His Father's pleasure over His life. Then at the beginning of Luke 4 we read that Jesus was led into the desert, and then the challenge of the devil starts. Luke 4:3 says, "The devil said to him, *'If you are the Son of God*, tell this stone to become bread' " (emphasis added).

Notice the devil's challenge: *"If* you are the Son of God." Just a few hours earlier the very voice of God had spoken over Him, "You are my Son." Now the devil challenges Jesus' relationship with God—the relationship that gives Him access to the authority of heaven. So often the same process happens in our lives. We receive a prophetic revelation endorsing our call and destiny as individuals or churches, and the next sound in our life is the negative challenge of the enemy: *"If* you are called to this city . . . *if* you are a preacher . . . *if* you are called to business . . ." And the doubt hits us! We need to speak with a new authority and confidence that declares to the spiritual realms: *"It is written—I* am!"

This is the battle of the wilderness; this is the fight of faith for our authority and destiny. We must believe that God called us to invade our streets and take the Word of God and root out the devil, breaking his power and establishing the Kingdom of God on our streets and in the marketplace once again. We are called; we are chosen for our generation; this is the hour of the Church, and the gates of hell will not prevail against us. We *are* the children of God with a mission to uproot and destroy the works of the devil on our streets! It is time to take Jesus' name onto the streets and believe the call of God on our lives to change our cities—this is the time for breakthrough!

In Luke 4:5–7 we see Satan directly challenge Jesus over the issue of authority:

> The devil led him up to a high place and showed him in an instant all the kingdoms of the world. And he said to him, "I will give you all their authority and splendor, for it has been given to me, and I can give it to anyone I want to. So if you worship me, it will all be yours."

In many ways this is so similar to the temptation that caused Adam and Eve to stumble, allowing sin to enter the world. In the Garden of Eden, the serpent seduced Eve by telling her that if she ate of the Tree of the Knowledge of Good and Evil, then she would have more power; she would have more influence and greater wisdom. She ate the fruit and swallowed the lie, and so opened the door of false power and authority. The temptation of

Satan now challenging Jesus all these years later was so similar, in effect saying, "Look, Jesus, I can give You power. I can give You influence, and it can all be Yours and You can be significant— You can have authority and please Yourself."

But the fact is, no authority was *ever given* to Satan, so he has no authority to give it to anyone else. He was not given authority; he stole it! He deceived Eve in the Garden and usurped her in order to get his authority. Then he turned and boasted to Jesus, "I have authority and I can give it to anyone I want to!" However, Jesus responded by saying, "It is written: 'Worship the Lord your God and serve him only'" (verse 8).

Jesus refused to cooperate with Satan's deception. "I will only ever worship the Father," He said. "I have a relationship with My God, and from that relationship will flow My source of authority." Jesus' authority worked the same way that parental authority works in any family—through relationship. Dad may be at work all day, but the children know that because of the relationship between Mom and Dad, they had better behave. Even though Mom might be small, she still has powerful authority because of her relationship with the children's dad. The relationship between Jesus, the Son of God, and His Father was so key, because no relationship would mean no authority! But Jesus knew who He was, and no demon in hell was going to rob Him of that relationship. In the same way, the Church needs to know who she is—the beloved Bride of Christ. We are chosen; we have a relationship with the Father through Christ, and from this place our authority flows. We need to know *whose* we are, not just *what* we are!

Jesus won the battle for His authority, and since He won this fight of faith, He was able to leave the place of temptation in the power of the Spirit with authority. As we continue to read, we see in Luke 4:36 that others also noticed this change in the effectiveness of Jesus: "All the people were amazed and said to each other, 'What is this teaching? With authority and power he gives orders to evil spirits and they come out!'"

People who listened to this new way Jesus talked began to marvel at Him. They were drawn by the obvious power and authority that He had. He simply ordered evil spirits to come out of people, and they did—just like that! Unsurprisingly, news about Jesus spread throughout the surrounding area as people told one another what they had seen.

One Jesus walked into the wilderness, but another Jesus came out of the wilderness with a different mantle, a different authority, a different way of speaking. He had such power and authority that a whole geographical area began to talk about Him. I believe this is what God wants to restore in the Church—a sound of authority and a power that is so evident that when we speak and minister to people, whole areas are affected; the community marvels and the media begins to comment because they are witnessing an authority that has the power to change people's lives and situations. When at last what we speak out comes to pass, the people who witness it will have a new respect for the Church, rather than an attitude of cynicism and mockery. It is time for the Word of God to be in our mouths and for something to happen when we speak!

In Matthew 9:6–8 we read about an occasion where Jesus heals a paralytic man, and again the people are amazed:

> Then he said to the paralytic, "Get up, take your mat and go home." And the man got up and went home. When the crowd saw this, they were filled with awe; and they praised God, who had given such authority to men.

The last line of that verse is significant. Grasp this: God *has* given such authority to men. He has! I believe that God wants to pour out a fresh anointing of authority on His Church at this time. Not an authority that is overbearing or dominating, but an authority that is a sign in the spirit realm that causes awe and produces a right fear and reverence for God.

We read in the book of Acts that in the early Church amazing signs and miracles happened through the apostles. There were numerous wonders, and Acts 4:34 says that there was not a needy one among them; the believers all had one heart and mind. Outsiders looked at their lifestyle and frankly were blown away with how they lived. Many people were added to the Church during that time, but they came with a respect for the Church—they knew this was real and they could not play games with the presence of God.

God wants us to live like that, too—as a power-filled community with one heart, with one mind, walking in authority and seeing the boundaries of God's Kingdom constantly pushed forward. The world is tired of religious dogma, of trite Christian sayings and all our "glory hallelujahs," which are nothing more than a clichéd phrase we tag onto the end of sentences. But there is a great hunger in the world to listen to a message that has authority, that is full of life-changing power, that can tell them how to be transformed and has the power to back up the words that are spoken. Only a little while ago I was speaking to a young man, seventeen years old, who comes from a wealthy family who attends our church. He surprised me when he asked me, "Take me somewhere where I can feel and see the presence of God. I want to see it!" There is a hunger on the streets for the real thing, so we need a breakthrough of the power of God in our cities and churches—people are hungry to see a God-sized God in the Church!

The Bible holds the key to life. It deals with every issue of life imaginable and is full of power. But because the Church has lacked the authority to back up its teaching, our words have been empty and hollow. Meanwhile, the world has sought to teach itself. These days you can go and find a seminar on any topic you can think of and be taught life skills. There are seminars on how to deal with grief and stress, seminars on marriage, parenting, anger management and so on. But the Church needs to reclaim its role of teaching these life-giving truths from the Bible and challenge all of these human self-help programs that have taught people to cope with life independently of God. We need to show the world the God-factor again, which enables them to be what they want to be. The Word of God taught with authority changes lives! Let's get rid of all our religious jargon and dogma and ask God to anoint us with power. When our message is authentic, meaningful and transforming, then the people will flock to hear it; then we will get people's attention, just as Jesus did.

## A closer look at the word *authority*

As believers, we need to understand the sense of privilege and ability, the capacity and competency that God has conferred upon us as His representatives on the earth. We have been delegated responsibility and given a jurisdiction on earth to extend the Kingdom of our God. "Thy will be done on earth as it is in heaven" should be our heartcry.

A closer look at the word *authority* will help us to understand how expansive our influence is intended to be. Our English word *authority* comes from the Greek word *exousia*, which has a very broad, full meaning. It means "an ability, a privilege, a force, a capacity, a competency that comes upon a person."[1] Authority carries a sense of strengthening, which brings a freedom. It is mastery in a specific area. There is a sense that a person with authority is a craftsman, someone who is highly

1. *Strong's Greek Dictionary*, No. 1849, http://ulrikp.dk/strongsgreek/.

skilled. But authority is also a delegated influence. It has a definite jurisdiction and power. It has strength and it has rights.

I believe that we now need to use our authority as the Church and repossess the "gates" of our enemies. We need to take back what the enemy has stolen from us! Like a policeman, we have been given a uniform in accordance with our rank and authority—we have been clothed with the Holy Spirit's power sent from on high. It is time we stopped walking the streets of our cities as observers, watching the oppression of the enemy, and lifted our badges of authority to use the power that has been given to us. We need to put up our hands and say "Stop!" to the influence of the enemy on our streets.

If a policeman in uniform is walking along the street, we will usually notice him, but we do not respond unless he signals to us to do something. But if a police officer says "Stop!" to us, then we know we have to respond! In spiritual terms, we have that same kind of authority, but if we do not take action or speak to the spiritual powers controlling the people, life will just go on as before. We must begin to use the authority given to us to stop the work of the devil.

## City gates—the place of influence

In biblical times every city had a wall around it that gave the city protection. It was only possible to enter the city through a number of gates. Jerusalem had twelve gates at different points around the city. These "city gates" were known as places of influence where the elders of the city sat and made judgments about the life of both the people and the city. The elders had authority and were able to make executive decisions that affected the lives of ordinary people. Because the gates were the only entry points into the city, the elders could decide what came in and out. They could determine what influences or products were allowed in. Equally, they could expel and rid the city of anything they considered negative.

I believe that our modern-day cities still have walls around them and gates that are points of entry, only now these are spiritual walls and gateways and are not as easy to identify as the natural entry points of historic cities. These spiritual gates need to be reclaimed and occupied by the Church as key places of influence that affect what comes into and goes out of the city. They are doors of influence that define the atmosphere and the value systems of the city. These gates control the way in which people live; they identify and define the priorities of the city and community. Examples of city gates would be education, teaching and training, health and medical care, finance and banking, theater, drama, the arts, media, politics, government and local legislation, the Church, family, social security and welfare, plus many other doors of influence and power. All these gates are controlled by people in the city, many of whom have little or no concept of God. The Church needs to occupy these gates with godly, Spirit-filled men and women who are able to discern what should be allowed in and what should be expelled from the city.

In Genesis 22:17–18 God gave an incredible promise to Abraham—one that I believe, as Abraham's seed, holds true for us today:

> "I will surely bless you and make your descendants as numerous as the stars in the sky and as the sand on the seashore. Your descendants will take possession of the cities of their enemies, and through your offspring all nations on earth will be blessed, because you have obeyed me."

God promised that because of Abraham's obedience, generation after generation would be raised who would take possession of their enemy's cities and possess the gates. The same promise is reiterated in Genesis 24:60: "And they blessed Rebekah and said to her, 'Our sister, may you increase to thousands upon thousands; may your offspring possess the gates of their enemies.'"

And again in Psalm 127:5, speaking of raising up godly children, we read, "Blessed is the man whose quiver is full of them. They will not be put to shame when they contend with their enemies in the gate."

We are called to raise a generation of sons and daughters who will possess these city gates with divine authority delegated by God. As parents, we have the incredible privilege of raising our children with both a natural and a spiritual expectation to have influence in their city. I believe that those born to us should arise with a warrior spirit and know that they carry the power of God on their lives as they contend for their rightful place in the gates. I believe it is time to raise confident children to go to work in the marketplace, knowing that they can serve God effectively in business and also raise those who will work in the Church. For too long Christian parents have felt that secular employment is a secondary calling, wanting their children's primary involvement to be inside the Church. But I pray that our children will possess the city gates!

Over the last few years, many of us have cried out to God in intercession and asked Him to bring change in our societal institutions: in education, health, the legal system and other areas of city life. These prayers have made an impact, and we can see the harvest of Christians being raised to positions of authority in these institutions. Working from the inside out, God is putting people of influence into strategic places in the city gates. But if we now fail to raise the next generation of leaders to take their place, then even if we win our battles and possess the gates today, what will happen when this present generation dies? One of the great tragedies of the Church is that we have seen many revivals and awakenings touch communities, but they come and they go. Then we lose the ground of influence because we fail to raise up the next generation to guard the ground we have taken. After a season of successful occupation where we have watched the Kingdom of God have an impact, we have often relinquished the gates to the enemy once more, and a new generation has had to start the battle all over again! This time we must work together. Let us raise our sons and daughters to be great prayer warriors, full of power and authority, who will possess the gates and know how to keep occupation of the land when we pass them the baton.

## Possession

I love the full meaning of the word *possess* in this context. The Abrahamic promise was for generations of descendants to "possess the gates of the city." *Possess* has a much broader meaning than our simple English definition, which means "to inherit." In its fullest sense it means "to go to the gate and cast out," "to expel," "to totally ruin," "to drive out every trace of," "to seize upon," "to overturn," and "to succeed in the place of and make room for yourself."[2]

That is how we are to possess the enemy's gates. There are to be no nice peace talks, no politically correct truces. This is outright warfare. We, the people of God, are to totally cleanse and purify the gates of all the false authority that the enemy has in that area of community life. We are to expel him, eradicate every trace of his activity and succeed in taking possession of that area completely and utterly. Then we are to seize the gate

2. Greek word *katecho*, *Strong's Greek Dictionary*, No. 2722, http://www.sacrednamebible.com/kjvstrongs/STRGRK27.htm.

and rout the enemy, eventually sitting down and making a comfortable space for the principles of God to come and rule! The Kingdom of God should come and sit down and influence our cities.

## "Believing" authority

God said to me once while I was praying, "Possession is a word of authority. I am calling you to take hold of enemy territory and mark it as your own. I am calling you to a spiritual battle to regain your authority and take back what has been taken from you."

Authority has to be mixed with faith. God gives authority to those who believe. Faith and authority are like an engine and a train carriage coupled together—they are designed to function together in partnership. So authority is a *believing authority*. We see this in Mark 16:17–18:

> "And these signs will accompany those who believe: In my name they will drive out demons; they will speak in new tongues; they will pick up snakes with their hands; and when they drink deadly poison, it will not hurt them at all; they will place their hands on sick people, and they will get well."

To those who believe the promises of God, authority is given. The Lord commanded Joshua to lead His people across the Jordan River into the Promised Land and promised him, "I will give you every place where you set your foot, as I promised Moses" (Joshua 1:3). I believe that God is calling us to take our feet outside the Church doors and begin to possess the enemy's gates with authority. God is looking for a people who will press in and utterly ruin, destroy and overthrow the work of the enemy and take possession of these gates of our communities.

In every historic revival that truly influenced the city and social life, we find this transition happened: People began to speak and affect the gates of health, education and finance, and then these areas of influence were repossessed by the people of God. Classic examples are Wesley, Wilberforce and Lord Shaftesbury—men who broke through in the Spirit and enabled a transference to take place from the Church to society. Wilberforce possessed the gate of justice for the slaves, and Shaftesbury possessed the gates of children and family and so changed the face of English culture. Many of the principles they fought for changed the very legislation of the land and are still part of our basic laws today. Wilberforce crusaded against slavery, and the resulting laws still govern us today; we are still living in the inheritance of what God did through him.

Rees Howells, one of the leading intercessors after the Welsh revival, also spoke about "gaining positions of authority." Howells taught that he prayed until he saw a breakthrough in the heavenlies, but he did not stop there; he continued praying until he saw the result on earth. He prayed until he could see the effect of his prayer and appropriate that victory on earth; he became a lightning conductor that drew down the answer of prayer from heaven to earth.

Omar Cabrera, one of the grandfathers of the Argentinean revival in prayer and intercession, once said, "I pray until the glory comes down or the devil manifests." In other words, he looked for a confrontation or manifestation on earth that told him he had won in the heavenly realm. Over a period of 27 years, God enabled him to have a tremendous impact on ninety cities. Omar said that as his authority and faith in prayer grew, he was able to go into a city for a few days and wrestle in the place of prayer with the spiritual powers and atmospheres present in that geography and find he was increasingly effective in changing the environment. Literally, when he then went to preach in the same city, he would find the demons would shriek and manifest quickly, souls would be hungry to get saved and miracles and healings would break out like popcorn. He knew that with God's help he could lay siege to a city in prayer and wage war in the spiritual realm with godly authority to see curses over the land broken and rescue the people.

Having authority is useless if you do not then use it. We need to pick up our authority with faith and go out and lay hands on the sick; we need to place our feet on our ground and possess it. We see this in the apostle Paul's life. When he walked into a city, his very presence would challenge the spirit realm. He knew he had authority over the evil spirits and so used the Word of God mixed with faith to address the powers of darkness in various cities. Consequently, he was often unpopular! People did not like Paul because he challenged spirits of false prophecy, divination, sorcery and sexual immorality. He rebuked them, destroyed their power and saw the Kingdom of God come to many cities he visited. Paul became a nuisance as he challenged the ungodly economies that functioned because of the witchcraft and sexual sin. No doubt many businessmen hated Paul! He changed atmospheres and, by the power of the authority on his life, changed the spiritual climate of the city.

As I have dwelt upon these things over the years, God has changed some of my theology and my understanding of the power of prayer in the context of spiritual warfare. God has shown me that effectiveness in spiritual warfare has more to do with having faith in our position of delegated authority in the name of Jesus than about the actual words we speak or the style of praying we do. In other words, our success in changing the atmosphere of our city has more to do with our *position* than our *confession*. It is related more to our character and standing than our sound and our language.

In recent years there has been much more understanding concerning the spiritual power of confession. We understand the power of speaking out and claiming God's promises. We have realized that ungodly, critical, negative attitudes are destructive, and our words have power—both the negative and positive words we speak. There is some truth in the statement, "What you say is what you get." We have realized that if we create a negative, complaining atmosphere with our words, then like the children of Israel we, too, will live in a wilderness and experience the struggle of having just enough to survive. But you can confess all the "right," positive promises you like and it will not make a scrap of difference to your life if you are standing on a compromised lifestyle made of sinking sand! You can do all the right kind of talking and even pray in Jesus' name, and the devil will not budge an inch if you are not positioned correctly, making consistent godly choices for your life. Unless you are positioned for godly authority, you have no mandate to reclaim territory from the devil. But if you know you are living in obedience to God and honoring Him, you have every right to storm the enemy's territory, to challenge, cleanse and occupy it, pushing the enemy out and then moving the presence of God in!

For example, we may call a prayer meeting because we have just heard that a new nightclub is to be built opposite the church, or a new sex shop is to open in our town. We have prayer meetings where people will stand and pray passionately against the tide of sexual immorality and filth in society. All the right kinds of confession and declaration are made. We cry out to God, but are we able to pray with true authority? Are we in the right spiritual position ourselves to take that ground? The enemy is never going to relinquish the ground of sexual sin to the Church if there is sexual sin in the Church! We have no authority to take this territory if, when we leave the prayer meeting and go home, we later find ourselves "relaxing" by watching a film where the storyline is full of adultery and sex. If we watch and enjoy the sexual stuff for our leisure, how can we have any real authority against this atmosphere in our city? We will never take that ground if we find ourselves reading novels that stimulate our sexual fantasies or if we explore the Internet for pornographic sites in our private lives! The devil laughs at our prayers against immorality when we ourselves do not have our lives correctly disciplined sexually. In order to be effective, we must be correctly positioned, submitted to the authority and holiness of God. If you are not living in the right place sexually, then you have no right to make declarations about taking that ground.

Now is the time for the people of God to live what we speak, to be holy and grow up. We need to seek purity and make sure we are standing on holy ground. If we need help, we need to cry out and realize our desperate need for God's mercy and grace. As James 4:6 reminds us, "God opposes the proud but gives grace to the humble."

Whenever we come to God with an attitude of pride in our prayers, like the Pharisee who said, "God, I thank you that I am not like other men—robbers, evildoers, adulterers" (Luke 18:11), God in His righteousness has to lift His hand of opposition to us and our pride. He cannot bless us. We need to forsake our pride and come to God on our knees. *The army that wins the victory will be on its knees in humility and holiness before God.* If you come in humility, then the hand that had to oppose your pride can actually bless you, for God gives grace to the humble. The very next verse in James says, "Submit yourselves, then, to God. Resist the devil, and he will flee from you" (verse 7).

If you are submitted to the Word of God in your life, humbled under the mighty hand of God, then you will be able to "resist the devil," and he must "flee from you." The very act of positioning your life in humility and submission under the hand of God is a mighty act of spiritual warfare.

If we have not positioned ourselves properly under the hand of God, then so many of our prayers will be ineffective, and this type of spiritual warfare can even become dangerous. If you are challenging the devil and his works without the full protection of God over your life, then you are in an exposed place. Before we stand up and decide to challenge one of the enemy's gates, we need to examine ourselves, look at our life-style and assess our level of obedience and authority in that area. This brings us full circle to the Scripture I quoted at the beginning of the chapter: "Jesus I know, and I know about Paul, but who are you?" (Acts 19:15).

The sons of Sceva knew all the right words to use, but they were completely lacking in authority. Look at what happened to them in the next verse: "Then the man who had the evil spirit jumped on them and overpowered them all. He gave them such a beating that they ran out of the house naked and bleeding" (verse 16).

We may not realize it, but that has happened to the Church on many occasions. We have had mighty prayer meetings, but the enemy has laughed at us and, even worse, lashed out at individuals. We cannot pray great authoritative prayers if we are not under the authority of God's Word in that area of our lives! It may sound very impressive but the devil does not move an inch and just laughs; we hear the sound of mocking: "Who are *you*?"

## Where are the gates of your city?

Having made the decision to examine our lives and live right, we now need to look at our city. What are the gates of your city that is God speaking to you about? For me, the gate of health is so important. I want to see the Church moving back into this gate and taking back possession of the territory of healing. I want to see the people of God sitting in this gate and watching the area of medicine and miracles come together. I value the medical profession very much. I have been incredibly blessed by the wisdom and expertise of doctors in my own life. But I believe it is time that the Church entered the health gate again and challenged society's skeptical attitude toward healing. We need to see both prayer and medicine working together; we need both the natural and the spiritual in partnership! I do not want the government's national health program or private health care companies to be the final authority in the gate of health; I want it to be the Church as she prepares the way for healing in our nations!

What about the other gates of finance, law and order, education, media, arts, youth, family, social services and many others? Which gate is God speaking to you about? What is your passion in the community? There is a cry in the Spirit that is calling us to possess the gates. Remember that the word *possess* means to inherit, cast out, seize, drive out and remove anything that should not be there, and then to sit, take residence and succeed in it utterly.

As you take a moment to consider your community and the influences that affect its value systems and atmosphere, ask God, "What is the sound You want to be released?" What should the Church be declaring? Many believers know they are being called to take an active part in their local schools and are becoming school governors; others are visiting their local councils and offering help. A lady I know has won favor with her local police force and town council, and she even has some local government funding for her church's projects, because she obeyed the call to step into the gate of youth for her community and began to pray. Having acted on their prayers, her church now runs an effective program to rescue young people from addiction, having set up a rehabilitation center to minister to those being ravaged by drug abuse, alcohol abuse and other addictions. God is really blessing their work. It is time for the Church to step into the city gates and rout the enemy.

So I challenge you to take some time to ask God to show you the gates of your community where His authority has been usurped and ask Him to show you what needs to be reclaimed by the people of God. Ask the Holy Spirit to direct you to where you need to go and possess the land.

Here is some encouragement from Psalm 24:1–4:

> The earth is the LORD's, and everything in it,
>     the world, and all who live in it;
> for he founded it upon the seas
>     and established it upon the waters.
>
> Who may ascend the hill of the LORD?
>     Who may stand in his holy place?
> He who has clean hands and a pure heart,
>     who does not lift up his soul to an idol
>     or swear by what is false.

Verse 1 affirms the fact that *everything* is the Lord's. We need to know that everything—every area of government, commerce, education, every local council—belongs to God. Everything. But again God is looking at our intentions, our attitudes. He is not looking at what we say; He is looking at our lives. If we have clean hands and a pure heart, then we qualify for the promise that continues in verse 5: "He will receive blessing from the LORD and vindication from God his Savior."

If you seek to position yourself correctly, to stand in the right place, then God will be with you and bless you. I pray that as you come to Him, seeking to take back the territory that the enemy has stolen, He will train your hands for battle and pour out upon you a fresh authority, so that you can lay hold of the promise given to Abraham and his descendants to possess the gates of your enemy. Then we need to train others to pass through those gates after us so that we see the banner of the King of Glory lifted high, our cities changed and the presence of Jesus on our streets again! It is a season of change and time for breakthrough—a time to turn back the enemy at the gates of our communities and a time for a new boldness on the Church.

# Leave the Keys of Breakthrough

As we stand in these city gates and watch the atmosphere of our communities change, and we see the answer to our prayers beginning to break through in tangible ways, a new cry begins to stir. This cry says to the next generation, "Please, do not drop the baton; maintain this breakthrough! Will someone carry my passion to the next generation? Please take my place so that the enemy cannot reoccupy these gates and steal our breakthrough!" Surely we cannot be fully satisfied just watching life change for us. We must be a turning generation that changes the flow of life for generations to come.

## Now run your race

If this is going to happen, then we need to grasp hold of the people around us and encourage them to take their place and run the race of their God-given purpose. Often, at an end of a meeting, someone will come to me and say, "I don't really know what I should be doing for God." It seems that too often we readily accept a passive Christian life and rationalize our frustration with the thought that as long as we are not causing anyone too much grief, we're doing okay. But then you have those occasional "God encounters" that trigger your real desires and awaken dreams that you thought you had buried. It is this deep sense of destiny we need to stir in others. It seems that too many have lost their sense of the Kingdom purpose of God for their life and lost sight of the fact that He desires to satisfy us and move us into the destiny plan He has prepared for us.

Hebrews 12:1–3 provides us with the antidote. God wants us to know that there is a race marked out for us—a specially prepared pathway of satisfaction! Cheered on by all those who have gone before us, we need to find our path and run with perseverance.

> Therefore, since we are surrounded by such a great cloud of witnesses, let us throw off everything that hinders and the sin that so easily entangles, and *let us run with perseverance the race marked out for us.* Let us fix our eyes on Jesus, the author and perfecter of our faith, who for the joy set before him endured the cross, scorning its shame, and sat down at the right hand of the throne of God. Consider him who endured such opposition from sinful men, so that you will not grow weary and lose heart.
>
> emphasis added

I have a vivid memory of a church service that changed my life. A preacher walked into the meeting. He was a normal-looking, dark-haired man wearing a suit. He was not a particularly charismatic character, or humorous for that matter, so as a seventeen-year-old pretty unimpressed by this visitor, I did not give him much attention. However, as soon as this man opened his mouth and began to preach, I knew that this message was going to be very different from the numerous others I had heard growing up as a minister's kid. There was a passion about this man that was captivating. His words made an impact and challenged me. In fact, his very first statement provoked me, and from then on he had my full attention. He made this statement: "Many are called, but few are making the choice that will help them fulfill their calling."

It is true. We all have a calling—a clear, individual, God-given purpose—and yet few of us have the courage to keep making the consistent choices that will enable us to be in the right place at the right time so that we completely fulfill our purpose. I had known since I was a little girl that I only wanted to do what God had created me to do. I always had a strong sense of wanting to fulfill my destiny, to do my best and to go for the gold. But suddenly, as I listened to this preacher, I realized that if I was going to get to where God wanted me to be, I was going to have to make definite, even costly, decisions.

Each one of us is born with God's fingerprints of destiny inside us, but it takes a lot of discipline to make consistent, tough decisions, so that everything within us is released for purpose. Yet if we would only take action, we would turn our potential into reality. One of the saddest things in the world is to walk through a graveyard knowing that many of the headstones mark the place where a person lies buried along with their unfulfilled potential. You can only stop and wonder what happened to all those dreams that died and what the world would look like now if they had lived their dreams. It is time for the people of God to live their dreams and not just journal them and keep dreaming. We need to take hold of them and run! As God's children, we should know how to take hold of our dreams more than anyone else. We, of all people, possess the ability to live them empowered by the Holy Spirit.

Looking further at this first verse of Hebrews 12, phrase by phrase, will help us to understand how to take hold of this principle and apply it to our lives so that we see the super-natural breakthrough we long for.

## Therefore

Why do Bible verses often begin with "therefore"? This word occurs whenever the writer wants to let us know that the statement he is about to make is a conclusion of what has previously been stated. So, in order to understand the "therefore" at the beginning of Hebrews 12, we need to look back and find the key in chapter 11. Hebrews 11 is dedicated to the "heroes of the faith." It recounts the personal stories of men and women who have run their race and now have taken their place in history as people of faith who endured the challenges set before them and achieved their God-given goals. Having given this roll call of honor, the writer of Hebrews then turns to us and says, "You've read about all these heroes of the faith, but what about you?" He challenges us: "Therefore, since we are surrounded by such a great cloud of witnesses..." In other words, "Look at all these people who went the distance and finished their course. It's up to you now. It's your turn to run the race and achieve something for God."

Just like the crowd of spectators at an Olympic event, the "cloud of witnesses" is cheering us on. In these days I believe the Church is beginning to grasp a sense of the value of our history, and it is stirring the challenge of our destiny like never before. We have the sense that heroes of the faith like John and Charles Wesley, George Whitefield, Smith Wigglesworth and countless other great men and women of God in history are cheering us on from the grandstand of heaven, longing for the people of God today to be and to do all they can. I can almost feel the frustration as they exhort us, "Come on, Church! You were born for so much more than this! Run the race marked out for you! Pick up the baton and run!"

The grandstand of heaven is appealing to the worldwide Church, but especially, I believe, to the Church in the West, challenging us to get up, to wake up, to stop being so politically correct and to start doing what we were born to do. There has been an atmosphere of fear and apathy in the Western Church that has diluted our ability to give clear views and take definite action when needed. We have tended to sit back and try to blend into the background. I call this attitude the "urge to merge"! Our policy has been to keep our heads down and not cause any trouble. But this needs to change!

Just as the great cloud of witnesses who have gone before us have set us an example of courage and focus, so now we need to take our position in our time in history and do what we are called to do, both individually and corporately. There will always be this partnership, since the Church cannot do what it is meant to do corporately if we are not doing what we are gifted to do individually. This does not mean that we each "do our own thing" with a selfish attitude of personal success, but we give ourselves wholeheartedly to our purpose so that the wider purposes of God for His Church will also be fulfilled. We position ourselves with hard work and sacrifice so that the Church can be positioned for victory and prominence!

## Cloud of witnesses

I believe that we need to look back and be provoked by the past. This is why the Bible gives us so many details of the journey of those who have run the race before us. We need to look and learn from both the positive and the negative legacies that history has recorded. We are privileged in the West to live in nations that have essentially Christian foundations. We need to honor and value this legacy and reawaken some of the values that have been lost over time. In the United Kingdom, much of the basis and reference points for the laws of the land came from our Christian heritage. The Church was responsible for starting educational programs for children and the poor; it was responsible for caring for the sick and establishing schemes that gave birth to the modern-day health system. All the great institutions that exist in Western culture today had the Church as their foundation stone...once. Sadly, over time the Church's influence has vacated these institutions, and we have watched humanistic and secular values infiltrate them. We have sat back and done nothing, and even foreign gods and other religions have moved in and demanded their place of influence in our nations. I believe the spectators gathered in the grandstand of heaven are shouting at us, "Enough! Wake up and take your place again; establish your authority again!"

At the Olympic Games in Greece, I remember watching as the television cameras panned across the exuberant crowd. The grandstand was filled with people who were there to support their country's athletes by yelling, waving and exhorting them to do their best. Although they were enthusiastic in their support, the vast majority of these people had never set foot on an athletics track and would probably never do so. They were simply spectators. In the great grandstand of heaven, however, every person watching has run the race. They are all former runners who are holding a gold medal! Imagine now the Olympic stadium full of ex-professional athletes with an insider's knowledge of the sport, cheering on the runners on the track, and then you have a more accurate picture of what heaven's cloud of witnesses looks like. They know exactly what they are cheering us for.

We need to stir ourselves again by reading the stories of some of the heroes of the past and allow ourselves to be challenged afresh by their example. Whenever you can, study the lives of people of greatness who answered God's call for their generation and fulfilled their purpose. Albert Einstein once said, "Rather, seek to be a man of values than a man of success." As we begin to understand the heartbeat and value systems of some of the heroes of faith, it will challenge the way we think, too.

These heroes have left their legacy and joined the ranks of heaven, but they have handed the baton to us. They are cheering us on to take our place in history, too. The history makers of yesterday are challenging us to push forward the frontiers of tomorrow. We, the Church, have to ask ourselves some serious questions: Are we answering destiny's call? Are we fulfilling the dreams and purposes of God for our lives individually?

## Run the race marked out for you

What did the writer of Hebrews mean to convey through the idea of running a race? At the time of writing, the culture did not recognize running as an activity that had anything to do with leisure, pleasure or fitness. Running was a serious business, and it could cost you your life! Only later was competitive running established and formed the basis of the ancient Olympic Games. Until then, running was about communication. There were training schools where the most promising runners of the nation were gathered and trained further so they could run for endurance, carrying vital messages during times of crisis— for example, between one military commander and another during a time of war—or to carry an edict from a monarch to the cities of their nation.

These men were part of the army, specially selected for their ability to persevere and for their speed, and commissioned to faithfully deliver messages to wherever they were dispatched. Their whole reason for being was to run with endurance and fulfill their appointed task. This was the picture that the author of Hebrews had in mind when he described how we should run the race of faith. Those who read the epistle around the time it was written would have clearly understood its message: We must be like the highly trained messenger, resolute and totally focused on his purpose, ready to run tirelessly.

These runners knew that their task was to deliver a message that would influence the destiny of a nation. So when the Bible tells us, "Do you not know that in a race all the runners run, but only one gets the prize? Run in such a way as to get the prize" (1 Corinthians 9:24), the words carry the weight and gravity of the fact that we run with the destiny of a nation hanging in the balance. This is not like the parents' race on sports day at our children's school. We carry a message that can save our nation from calamity! Often these runners would run until the point of death to achieve their mission. They would run without stopping, taking no food or water in extreme circumstances, and were expected literally to lay their lives down for the cause of the message. Over great distances the men would run in relays, and so their task was often to hand on the message to the next person to ensure that it reached its destination. In the same way, each one of us has a huge responsibility to run our section of the race as if we were the only person who could do it—as if it all depended on us. But we also run to ensure that when our personal race is over, we hand the message on to others who themselves have trained and prepared to run *their* leg of the race.

While we run as individuals, it is clear that we must also run as a team. We are in a relay race for the spiritual destiny of our nations! Across our nations I believe God has set up a race of faith that is being directed by the Holy Spirit. It spans generations, gender, denominations and ethnicity. But now we must take our place and run our part with a sense of urgency and responsibility. We must run, overlooking our personal preferences and even weariness for the sake of our nation. We must run with an attitude of excellence.

## Let us throw off everything that hinders

There are many things that can hinder us both individually and corporately, but I want to focus on one particular issue. There exists an attitude of *independence* that characterizes so many of the runners in this great race of faith. Many runners appear unable to discern when it is time to release their baton of vision to another, or indeed, when to position themselves to get ready to take hold of it and run.

In the Olympic Games, the men's 4 × 100 meters is always a highlight and is fiercely competitive. In the 2004 Summer Olympics held in Athens, the U.S. relay team was feared and revered by all the other countries because it contained so many great runners, including that year's gold-medal-winning 100-meter runner, Justin Gatlin, and the bronze medalist, Maurice Green (also a three-time gold medalist at 100 meters). They were literally known as the "team of the superheroes"!

The British team, on the other hand, comprised a much more inauspicious lineup. It included Darren Campbell, who, earlier in the games, had failed to complete one of his races in the individual events due to injury. There was therefore much criticism and speculation about whether he should even have been included in the relay team. As the teams lined up for the final, on paper it looked as though the Americans would cruise to certain victory. As the commentators discussed the race before it started, most of the discussion centered on who they thought would come in the silver and bronze positions, as they all thought that the United States would certainly take the gold. However, history recorded an astounding victory for the British underdogs!

I was in America at the time of the games, and it was fascinating to pick up and read the accounts of the race in the U.S. newspapers. The headline of one read like this:

Superheroes Beaten by Good Teamwork. At the time God used that statement to speak to me powerfully. It struck me that it was time for the Church to work as a team and run to win! No one expects the Church to make a dramatic impact any longer. The Church is the underdog, and its relevance to life is overlooked. But the Church needs to arise and run. We need to throw off *everything* that hinders us. We need to learn to work as a team; we need to practice slick and efficient baton changes between congregations and their leaders for the sake of the nations.

Although we may have incredible, anointed people in the Church, unless they are prepared to function in cooperation with others, they will not win the race. Those who truly win are those who work in cooperation with others. The individual statistics of the American team were incredible—as individuals, their achievements for their nation were outstanding. But when it came time to run as a team, they lost to a group of less impressive individuals, but individuals who had practiced as a team, had perfected their race and were committed to working together for their goal of the gold medal.

We need to get rid of every excuse that would hold us back from achieving our destiny and purpose in God. We must answer the call and throw off every mindset that hinders us from obeying God.

## The "middle" runners

Just as athletes have specialty events, so we need to run the specific part of the race for which God has gifted us. In a relay race there are four runners. Usually you find that it is the first and the last runners in a relay team that receive all the media attention. That's because one is responsible for getting a good start to the race and the other is responsible for completing that all-important final leg and crossing the finish line. Often we struggle to recall who it was that ran the second and third legs of the race even if the team wins! Yet they are absolutely vital to the success of the team as a whole. The second and third runners have to be both good receivers *and* good releasers, as they have to negotiate two baton changes. They have to be good team players, able to both receive and pass on the baton. They must watch closely the people they are running with and know when to run from their mark, ready to take the baton. They carry the huge responsibility of having a double chance of dropping the baton and fouling up the race!

In the Western Church, we have had many starters who have run the first leg of the race—many visionaries who carry a vision for a new era in the Church. But unfortunately many of them have not built strong relationships with others' gifts and have not been able to transfer efficiently their baton to the next runners. I believe we need to develop partners who can learn how to receive the baton from these visionary men and women, who are then able to develop the practical structures of these visions and in turn pass the baton on. So much has happened in recent Church history: We have seen the Father's blessing sweep across our nations, the G12 cell movement emerge for church growth and believers pray and forge links with the marketplaces of society. Each one of these initiatives now needs to have anointed "middle runners" take the baton so that the vision continues to the next stage. If this does not happen, then we face the danger that these gifts to the Church will become irrelevant, out of step or stagnant. With the help of middle runners, there is hope that we will actually adapt and expand upon what God has initiated.

There are so many churches existing today that once had a revelation about something, started running well and then faltered through a lack of middle runners. Maybe it was a vision to have an exceptional children's ministry or to build a community center. Whatever it was, they began running well but did not have the relational teamwork to stay the distance and see the race through to the end.

Why do we not finish our races well? Often I think it is because we do not understand the necessity of the second and third legs of the relay race. Everyone gets excited about fresh, new initiatives, and it is so satisfying to see something reach its logical conclusion—a dream fulfilled. But how many are prepared to work to see the middle ground covered? This is the least exciting part, maybe even boring and routine, yet so vital to the success of the whole venture. The middle part of the race is where the structure of the whole really begins to take shape. This is where the sheer hard work is done. For the projects we are involved in, this part represents the practical contributions of administration and finances, team training and leadership growth—the basic bread and butter of our journey! How we need those who are prepared to run with determination and perseverance this section of the race, despite the fact that they know they will not be the ones getting all the glory. We need to throw off the mindset that tells us what we are doing is humdrum and average and run with endurance, realizing that our contribution is vital to overall success.

## Triathlon or beach volleyball?

My son loves sports, which means I have watched all kinds of sports with him that I would not otherwise have watched. The modern Olympic Games now encompasses a wide range of events that were not included years ago. Take beach volleyball, for instance. How did that get into the Olympics? How can a group of people jumping around on the sand in bikinis whacking a ball at each other be a real Olympic sport? I am sure those who are exponents of it will write to me and explain just how difficult it really is, but to me it looks all too easy!

Real endurance sports like the triathlon look to me much more like the kind of event that should be included in the Olympic Games. The stamina required for a triathlon is amazing. This race is all about perseverance and endurance over a long period. The athletes begin by plunging into the freezing cold sea and swimming for 1.5 kilometers (just short of a mile); then they emerge soaking wet and immediately jump onto their bikes to cycle for 40 kilometers (24 miles), usually uphill. Then after cycling they have to jump off their bikes and run a further 10 kilometers (6.2 miles).

The amazing part is this—whether you win at beach volleyball or the triathlon, you still get a gold medal! The prize is the same if you are competing in the event for which you were born to win. We simply need to know which event is our destiny and then compete, but often we are looking to join in the volleyball game so that we can avoid the hardships of the triathlon! The fact is, we have to run the race marked out for us, as the writer of Hebrews tells us. Whether we are called to an endurance race or a sprint, we have to run the race that God has made us to run. We have to throw off everything that might hinder us from achieving that purpose and not seek to take easy options. If we faithfully run our race, then at the end there is a gold medal for us—God will reward us.

## Running your race

So many times people ask me, "What should I be doing for God?" We seem to think that God's will for our lives must be doing something that is not obvious or that we will not naturally enjoy or discover. I like to think it is much simpler than we imagine. Maybe a better question to ask is, "What would I enjoy doing for God?" I believe that inside each of us, God has left a divine mark of purpose and a desire that will direct us into what we should be doing—if we just stop and trust our instincts and gifts.

We can often be distracted by the fashionable calls and new ministries that seem to gain prominence—i.e., prophetic evangelism, intercession, spiritual warfare—and if we are not careful, we try to run in a part of the race God never intended for us to run. Perhaps we have tried to be a marathon runner when we are actually meant to be a sprinter, or vice versa. Each of us needs to find our section of the race and run it faithfully before God.

As well as throwing off the spirit of independence, we also need to throw off the attitude of the mediocre as we run this race. Let's run our race to get the gold medal and not be satisfied with merely finishing. As the apostle Paul puts it, "Run in such a way as to *get the prize*" (1 Corinthians 9:24, emphasis added). In other words, run to win! We have a philosophy in Church culture that shows we often see how much we can get away with, rather than how much we can put in. We have even disguised this lack of excellence with a veneer of false humility: "I don't want to be over the top; I don't want to expect too much and be greedy!" But I believe there is a huge difference between excellence and perfectionism. God calls us to excellence and wants us to give our best. He wants us to go for the gold in our Christian lives.

To achieve the top prize in any sport, you need to have an attitude of dedicated commitment. Top athletes are usually people who constantly make sacrifices in order to be at the top of their game. I remember a friend of my daughter Nicola's. From a very early age it was obvious to everyone that this girl possessed outstanding athletic ability. At their school's sports day I used to watch her compete. She would finish a huge distance in front of all the other children. This girl had a choice to make about whether she would develop her athletic skills further. At first she did, and she very quickly progressed to run for her county and then competed nationally. Everyone wondered how far she would go. Would she go on to compete at the Olympic level? But suddenly she faded from the athletics scene and stopped competing for quite a while, before mysteriously returning to competition. No one seemed to know why this hiatus had occurred.

Some years later I met this girl again at one of Nicola's birthday parties and had the opportunity to ask her what had happened. She told me that she was faced with a choice. "I had to decide," she said, "how much athletics meant to me. I felt it was so unfair that I had to give up eating pizza, that I always had to go to bed early, that I had to get up at 5:00 A.M. every day to train. I just didn't want to do it anymore." She continued, "But then I came to the point where I realized that, if I wanted to be the best I could be at this, I had to make sacrifices. I realized that my life couldn't be like everyone else's." Today this girl is a superbly trained athlete competing at a very high level. I would not be surprised if one day I see her crossing the finish line to claim an Olympic gold.

The same is true for us in the Church. We have to decide: To what are we going to give our time? I am not saying that we should only be ministry focused and never spend time with our families; clearly that is wrong. I am not even saying that watching television is terrible! We must beware of being sucked into our leisure- and pleasure-driven society and losing our discipline. But if we are going to run in such a way as to get the prize, there needs to be a fresh commitment to sacrifice in our lives to achieve the purposes of God. We need to let the urgent promptings of the Holy Spirit motivate us to run as never before.

The more I read Scripture, the more I am convinced that God demands excellence from us. If you read even the very practical biblical account of how the Temple was designed and built, you can tell that God is seriously into detail and likes gold! He wanted the best for His temple! What does going for the gold in our Christian life mean? I believe God wants us to be good students of His Word; He wants us to take time out to listen to Him; He wants us to use our brains; He expects us to be excellent stewards of the resources He gives us. In short, He wants our lives for Him to be characterized by excellence.

## And the sin that so easily entangles

We so easily get entangled in sin! Worse still, we tend to have the attitude that it does not really matter if we do sin, because God will always forgive us. I am so grateful for the grace and mercy of God that gives us many second chances in life, but often as believers we live our lives to the lowest common denominator instead of aspiring to live holy lives. I believe God is challenging us in these days: If we want to run the race, we have to deal with the sin issue. We must call sin, sin, and not make excuses for our behavior.

To run the race of faith without dealing ruthlessly with the sin in our life is as ridiculous as expecting a 100-meter runner to compete wearing a ball and chain. We are not designed to run the race God has marked out for us with sin in our lives. We will never run efficiently, and our sin will constantly trip us up. All of us know people who once were running a great race, but sin entangled them and they had a bad fall. We must recognize our own weaknesses, stop covering them up and making excuses for them, and deal with the sin issues in our lives. Galatians 5:7 says, "You were running a good race. Who cut in on you and kept you from obeying the truth?"

It is a good thing to pause occasionally and look back over your life and assess how you once ran for God compared to how you run for Him now. If you have made good progress, praise God! But maybe you look back and realize you were once much more focused than you are now, that you were fulfilling the purposes of God for your life; but today, if you are honest, you are not running with the same sense of direction and determination. Through this verse the Holy Spirit challenges us, "You *were* running a good race. What has slowed you down?"

What is distracting you and me from running as God intended? Often it is the little things that escape our attention, rather than a major issue. Have we lost the revelation of God's love for us? Have we lost the desire to spend time in God's presence? Have we lost a bit of our hunger for the purposes of God? It is so easy to get distracted, and before you know it, life is passing you by.

## Running with perseverance

Probably the toughest of all competitive races are the long-distance ones, because they are as much a test of mental endurance as physical prowess. The Christian life is about going the distance, staying the course over time, completing our allotted number of laps without fading out and giving up. Sometimes the journey we have to make is not over friendly terrain. It is not the pristine athletics track but a rugged, unpredictable landscape we have to navigate. We plunge into freezing cold water; we toil up steep mountains; we go on long walks through a wilderness; we trudge through valleys. There are no ten-second wonders! But God wants us to run with perseverance. We have to commit ourselves to this race with all our might. The Holy Spirit is our coach. He will stand with us and train and prepare us to run this race.

So we must run with perseverance and take hold of our destiny and breakthrough. Look at the baton that God has placed in your hand and ask yourself, "What is the mandate of God for my life? How can I know a fresh breakout of His presence upon me? What is the wilderness that I long to see become a fruitful field? What is the cry that I must allow to become more desperate?" We need to be like Hannah and allow these passions to be expressed. We must allow this process of change to realign our priorities. We need to be like Joseph and walk the journey of our dreams through all difficulty. We must acknowledge the deep longings of our hearts and begin to allow the vision to draw us into new places of risk. We need to ask God to give us our keys of breakthrough so that we can see cities changed through prayer, people healed of their sicknesses, churches released with new Kingdom finance and the next generation empowered to win. This is the time for the Church to break through. We need to remember that little keys open big doors! Today God wants to place these keys into the hands of the Church, and He asks us to release them to the next generation. We need to leave these keys of breakthrough as our legacy. We want the next generation to run farther, dream bigger and achieve more quickly what we have struggled to see. This is the time for change, this is the time to dream and this is the time for supernatural breakthrough!

Disturb us, Lord, when
We are too well pleased with ourselves,
When our dreams have come true
Because we have dreamed too little,
When we arrived safely
Because we sailed too close to the shore.

Disturb us, Lord, when
With the abundance of things we possess
We have lost our thirst
For the waters of life;
Having fallen in love with life,
We have ceased to dream of eternity
And in our efforts to build a new earth,
We have allowed our vision
Of the new heaven to dim.

Disturb us, Lord, to dare more boldly,
To venture on wider seas
Where storms will show Your mastery;
Where losing sight of land,
We shall find the stars.

We ask You to push back
The horizons of our hopes;
And to push us into the future
In strength, courage, hope, and love.[1]

1. Attributed to Sir Francis Drake, 1577.

# About the Author

Rachel Hickson is an internationally respected prayer leader and Bible teacher with a recognized prophetic gift. She has developed prayer and prophecy training schools in which she teaches all over the world, and is in demand as a conference speaker.

At the age of 24 Rachel entered into full-time ministry alongside Reinhard Bonnke in Africa. After just six weeks in Zimbabwe she almost lost her life in a horrific car accident, but was miraculously healed by God after intercessors prayed for her day and night. This incident birthed in Rachel a desire to pray and to help others realize the full potential of connecting with almighty God through prayer.

After returning from Africa, Rachel and her husband, Gordon, pastored a group of four churches in North London, and it was during this time that God directed them to establish Heartcry Ministries with the call to train and equip people to be released into effective prayer and intercession for their communities, cities and nations. In 2005 God called Rachel and Gordon to leave London and be based in Oxford where Gordon is associate minister on the staff of St. Aldates Church.

Rachel travels internationally, visiting Europe, North America, Africa and India. Invitations come from various denominational backgrounds, and frequently from regional groups of city leaders where a passion for unity has brought the churches together to pray for a move of God in their area. Rachel and Gordon have a passion to see cities transformed through the power of prayer and evangelism. One of their projects links churches and prayer ministries across London, which has developed a city strategy called the London Prayernet (see www.londonprayer.net).

Rachel has been married to Gordon for over 26 years and they have two children: their daughter, Nicola, who is married to Tim Douglass. They were a part of the London Hillsong Church for four years but are now living in Australia as part of the staff at the Sydney Hillsong Church. Rachel and Gordon also have a son, David, who is studying at Loughborough University, United Kingdom.

# Heartcry Ministries Information

Heartcry Ministries was founded in autumn 1993. The vision of Heartcry can be summarized in the following statements:

- To be one of the prophetic teaching ministries that comes alongside churches to help them understand what God is saying to them individually and corporately. To help people understand their destiny and calling, and answer the call of God in their lives.

- To train, equip and teach people and churches how to release their Heartcry to God in prayer and intercession and to be part of raising a prayer army that will cry out to God for their cities and nations.

- To provide weekend retreats, seminars and conferences in cooperation with local churches, where people can identify their hidden Heartcry, and through teaching, prayer and encouragement, find faith and healing for the restoration of their souls.

- To release a Heartcry for change in the communities and help people connect and answer the Heartcry of their neighbors. To provide prayer information and other strategies that enable the local churches to connect with the Heartcry for justice, righteous government and the social needs in their city or nation.

Heartcry hopes to continue strengthening the Church and the people to hear the urgent call to prayer. Now is the time to pray and cry out for our land and continent and watch what God will do for us!

Heartcry Ministries
31 Orchard Road
Botley
Oxford
Oxfordshire
OX2 9BL

www.heartcry.co.uk
www.londonprayer.net

# What every prayer warrior needs to know—

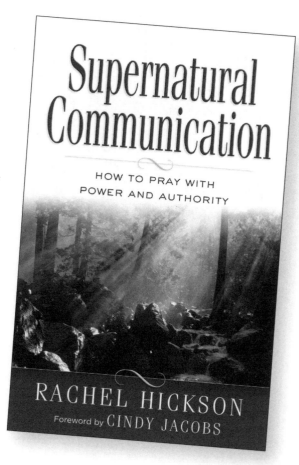

Learn to pray with power and authority by discovering your personal style of prayer!

Supernatural Communication

HOW TO PRAY WITH POWER AND AUTHORITY

RACHEL HICKSON

Foreword by CINDY JACOBS

"While there are a number of excellent books on the market on prayer, *Supernatural Communication* fills a need that none of them has touched."

—from the foreword by Cindy Jacobs

Start with page 124b - 125a
then 125b

page 135 *